AN UNOFFICIAL ENCYCLOPEDIA OF STRATEGY FOR FORTNITERS

DUOS AND SQUADS STRATEGIES

JASON R. RICH

Sky Pony Press
New York

Copyright © 2018 by Hollan Publishing, Inc.

Fortnite® is a registered trademark of Epic Games, Inc.

The Fortnite game is copyright © Epic Games, Inc.

Sky Pony Press books may be purchased in bulk at special discounts for sales promotion, corporate gifts, fund-raising, or educational purposes. Special editions can also be created to specifications. For details, contact the Special Sales Department, Sky Pony Press, 307 West 36th Street, 11th Floor, New York, NY 10018 or info@ skyhorsepublishing.com.

Sky Pony® is a registered trademark of Skyhorse Publishing, Inc.®, a Delaware corporation.

Visit our website at www.skyponypress.com.

10 9 8 7 6 5 4 3 2

Library of Congress Cataloging-in-Publication Data is available on file.

Cover design by Brian Peterson

Print ISBN: 978-1-5107-4342-7
Ebook ISBN: 978-1-5107-4343-4

Printed in China

TABLE OF CONTENTS

CHAPTER 1

DO YOU HAVE WHAT IT TAKES TO SURVIVE ON THE ISLAND?

*F*ortnite: Battle Royale from Epic Games continues to be one of the most popular games in the world. In addition to providing an overview of the game itself, this strategy guide focuses on the **Duos** and **Squads** game play modes, plus offers strategies for successfully surviving and winning many of the temporary, team-oriented game play modes that are offered within the game.

To get started, find a partner (or up to three other gamers to complete your squad), and get ready to take a trip to the mysterious island, where your high-action, combat-oriented adventure is about to unfold.

You can experience *Fortnite: Battle Royale* on a PC, Mac, Xbox One, Playstation 4, Nintendo Switch, Apple iPhone, Apple iPad, or Android-based mobile device. Regardless of which gaming platform you use, expect nonstop excitement and intense combat during each match you experience.

The challenges you're about to experience take place on a mysterious island. It's divided up into more than 20 main locations (referred to as *points of interest*). By looking at the island map, it's easy to see that located throughout the island are many labeled and unlabeled locations that offer interesting places to explore, as well as different types of terrain.

Each gamer who participates in a match controls one soldier who is transported to the island by a flying Battle Bus.

As the blue Battle Bus follows a random route over the island at the start of a match, each soldier decides when and where to leap from the bus in order to begin their freefall toward land. Displayed in the top-left corner of the screen are the Health and Shield meters for each member of your team or squad. All squad members should mark their chosen landing location on the map. A colored flare will be created, allowing the rest of the team to meet up at the marked location upon landing. Here, you can see these colored flares in the lower-right corner of the screen.

Using the directional controls on your game controller (or your mouse and keyboard), help your soldier navigate during their freefall.

Ideally, you want your soldier to reach your desired landing location as fast as possible, before enemy soldiers land in that same area. By pointing your soldier downward, you can increase their falling speed.

To ensure a safe landing, each soldier is equipped with a glider. The glider can be manually deployed at any time during the freefall. However, it automatically activates as a soldier gets close to land. Once the glider is activated, it slows down the soldier's rate of descent and gives gamers much more precise navigational control over their soldier's landing.

The moment each soldier lands on the island, there's just one overall objective—*survival*.

Upon landing, each soldier is armed only with a pickaxe and an empty backpack. The pickaxe can be used as a close-range weapon, but it's main purpose is to smash objects apart and to harvest resources (wood, stone, and metal) that need to be found and collected while on the island. These resources are used to build ramps, bridges, structures, and fortresses, as well as to purchase weapons and items from Vending Machines that are scattered throughout the island.

To survive for more than a few moments on the island, immediately upon landing, begin searching for and collecting weapons, ammunition, loot items, and resources. Ultimately, based on where you are on the island and what challenges you're facing at any given mode, it's important to choose the best weapon or tool to utilize.

Beware of the Deadly Storm

To make your situation on the island even more challenging, within minutes after the soldiers arrive at the start of a match, a deadly storm forms and begins to make large portions of the island uninhabitable.

As the storm expands and moves during each match, the remaining soldiers are forced to stay within the ever-shrinking eye of the storm (also known as *the circle*). This is the only safe and inhabitable terrain.

When viewing the island map, the area displayed in pink has already been engulfed by the storm and has become uninhabitable. The outer circle shows the storm's eye, which is currently the only land that continues to be safe. The inner circle shows where the storm will be expanding and moving to next.

It is possible to survive within the storm for short periods of time. However, for each second your soldier stays within the storm, their Health meter gets depleted. As the match progresses, the amount of damage per second incurred by remaining within the storm increases. Shields do not protect a soldier from the storm.

Each time the eye of the storm shrinks, the remaining soldiers are forced into closer proximity, until combat is the only option for anyone who hopes to survive.

Each time the storm expands and moves, it goes in a random direction (as opposed to just shrinking the eye of the storm).

Fight Alone, with a Friend, or as Part of a Squad

At the start of each **Solo** match, up to 99 other soldiers (each controlled in real-time by a separate player) are also transported to the island.

By the end of a match, only one soldier (or several members of a team or squad) will remain standing and achieve #1 Victory Royale. Everyone else will perish. There's no

second place. Each match lasts approximately 15 minutes, but this varies, based on the skill level of the players and how quickly the enemy soldiers are defeated. In the previous screen-shot, three out of four of the squad members survived and won the match. All enemies were defeated.

Fortnite: Battle Royale offers three permanent game play modes—**Solo, Duos,** and **Squads.**

The **Duos** game play mode allows two players to work together during a match in order to defeat up to 98 other gamers.

Squads mode allows teams of up to four gamers to become allies and work together in order to survive each match and defeat all enemy soldiers (up to 96 of them). Squads can be composed of four online friends, or you can have the game match you up with three random team members before a match begins.

Every week or two, Epic Games releases a game update (called a Patch), which often introduces one or more new, but temporary, game play modes into the game—many of which encourage teams to be formed and allies to be made.

Once you choose the Duos or Squads game play mode, you'll be able to see which of your online friends are logged into the game from the Party Finder menu. Any of these people can be invited to join you for a match. Otherwise, you can choose the Fill option, and have random players selected to become your partner or teammates.

Gamers Must Manage Multiple Objectives Simultaneously

With so much happening on the island at any given moment, survival requires gamers to juggle 10 main objectives and responsibilities simultaneously in order to stay alive. These include:

1. Safely exploring the island.
2. Avoiding the deadly storm.
3. Harvesting and collecting resources (wood, stone, and metal).
4. Finding, collecting, and managing a personal arsenal of weapons.
5. Locating and collecting ammunition for the weapons.
6. Acquiring and properly using loot items that can help a soldier survive.
7. Managing the inventory within their backpack (which only has six slots capable of holding weapons or loot items, in addition to the pickaxe).
8. Building ramps, bridges, structures, and fortresses using the collected resources in order to reach otherwise inaccessible places, or to provide defensive shielding during attacks.
9. Engaging in combat with enemy soldiers in order to become the last person standing at the end of a match.
10. Prepare for the End Game of a match (also referred to as the *Final Circle*), when the eye of the storm is very small, and only a few enemy soldiers remain alive.

When you opt to experience the Duos or Squads game play mode, you no longer have to face each of these objectives and responsibilities alone. But, whether you're playing with one team member in Duos mode, three other online friends in Squads mode, or you're experiencing one of the other game play modes that allows players to team up, working with allies in real-time requires two additional and extremely important responsibilities—*communication* and *strategy planning*!

As you'll discover, there are several ways for allies to communicate during each match. By working together, you must help each other stay alive. For example, you can pool resources as well as share weapons, ammo, and loot items. Most importantly, you can plan joint and simultaneous attacks, but your actions often need to be well coordinated and perfectly timed to be successful.

The in-game Quick Chat menu is one way you're able to communicate with your allies during a game. This is particularly useful if you're not using a gaming headset with a built-in microphone and can't communicate with your voice.

Being able to communicate with your allies will allow you to plan and execute complex survival and combat strategies, so you can all work together quickly, while protecting each other. Failure to communicate properly or work together on planned objectives will typically result in failure.

During a match, you can easily identify your team members because a white arrow appears over their heads, along with their username.

Anytime you're in close proximity to your teammates, you're able to exchange weapons, ammo, and loot items. To drop something for your teammate to pick up, access the Backpack Inventory screen and select what you want to drop to the ground. Press the Drop button on your controller/keyboard.

To Become an Expert Requires Practice!

Regardless of which *Fortnite: Battle Royale* game play mode you experience, one thing that is required to achieve success is practice —*a lot of practice*. This unofficial guide will give you the knowledge you need to win matches and become a well-rounded player, but to actually achieve victory, you'll need to master core gaming skills, and be able to use those skills at lightning fast speed.

A top-ranked *Fortnite: Battle Royale* player has become a pro at using the various types of weapons offered on the island and has also spent countless hours learning what each weapon is capable of, how much damage each can cause, and in which situations each weapon is most useful. They've also spent time learning to accurately aim and fire their weapons.

At the same time, pro gamers have perfected the art of building within the game and are able to create the structures they need extremely quickly. Knowing what needs to be done at any given moment is only part of the challenge. Being able to successfully accomplish each task fast is what separates good *Fortnite: Battle Royale* players from the best players.

When it comes to playing the Duos or Squads game play modes, the best *Fortnite: Battle Royale* teams have discovered ways to quickly and succinctly communicate in real-time with each other. Communication allows squad members to work well together in the most intense and fast-paced fighting situations.

Knowing the skill levels and personal game styles your teammates possess is always helpful, so you can anticipate each other's actions during a match, particularly during an intense firefight. However, the best teams also share common goals during matches, and each team member does everything within their power to achieve those pre-planned objectives.

Because *Fortnite: Battle Royale* is an online-based game, team members can be located virtually anywhere in the world, yet still communicate well and work together within the game. Once a match begins, each gamer's

soldier can stick together with their teammates, or separate and explore different areas of the island (with the plan for survivors to meet up prior to the End Game).

Before a match actually begins, while hanging out in the pre-deployment area, for example, determine the random route the Battle Bus will take by checking the island map, and then choose a landing location for the team. Next, decide where each player will travel to while on the island, and what their responsibilities will be.

Potential Team Strategies

Choose an overall team-oriented strategy that works for you and your teammates. Here are some potential options:

One strategy is to assign each team member a specific task early in a match. For example, one person is put in charge of collecting resources, while another gathers weapons and ammo. The third and fourth team members are put in charge of building and/or protecting the other team members by providing cover for them. Team members can share weapons, ammo, loot items, and resources as needed.

Another strategy is for team members to stick together and support each other throughout the match. All team members collect weapons, ammo, loot items, and resources, plus build as needed. Staying together allows the team to protect each other, gang up on individual enemy soldiers, or launch coordinated attacks on enemy teams or squads.

When a squad works together, one team member can lure enemies out in the open, while his or her other teammates hide, and then launch a coordinated surprise attack from multiple directions at the most opportune moment.

A third general strategy is for all teammates to go off on their own during the early stages of a match. Then, as the End Game approaches, the surviving team members meet up at a designated location to confront their final enemies together.

The drawback is that individual soldiers from your squad (including yourself) could encounter enemy squads traveling together, so you or your teammates will be outnumbered and likely outgunned if you're alone during an encounter. If you're injured, there will also be nobody around to Revive you if everyone on the squad goes their separate ways.

Fortnite: Battle Royale Is Continuously Evolving

To ensure Fortnite: Battle Royale continues to be exciting, fresh, and offer ongoing challenges every time you visit the island and participate in a match, the folks at Epic Games release a game update every week or two.

A typical update will include: new weapons and/or loot items being introduced; new (unlabeled) areas being added to the island; minor alterations being made to existing points of interest; and tweaks being made to what existing weapons and/or loot items are capable of. Occasionally, weapons or loot items are "vaulted," meaning they're removed from the game, but could be re-introduced into the game in the future.

On a daily basis, new soldier outfits, pickaxe designs, backpack designs (called back bling), glider designs, and emotes are made available from the Item Shop. These are used to customize the appearance of your soldier (but cost money). Some outfits and related items are rare or are only made available for a limited time. Anything purchased from the Item Shop is for appearances only and does not enhance the speed, strength, agility, or fighting capabilities of a soldier.

Each time something new is added to Fortnite: Battle Royale, a News screen is displayed when you launch the game. You can also visit www.epicgames.com/fortnite/en-US/news to discover what's new.

In addition to the weekly or biweekly updates, every three to four months, Epic Games kicks off a new game play season. In conjunction with a new season, a massive game update is released.

At the start of a new season, major new points of interest (like Paradise Palm) are added to the map, and pre-existing points of interest are dramatically altered or removed altogether. Additional changes are also made to other aspects of the game, and a new Battle Pass begins (which offers a series of daily, weekly, and tier-based challenges).

Fortnite: Battle Royale Is Free to Play

One of the things that most gamers love about *Fortnite: Battle Royale* is that it's free! Anyone, using any popular gaming platform, can download and install the game, and play on an unlimited basis for free. However, in-game purchases are required if you want to acquire items from the Item Shop, purchase a Battle Pass, or unlock Battle Pass tiers (without completing the challenges associated with each tier).

PC and Mac users can visit www.Fortnite.com and click on the Download button (displayed in the top-right corner of the web browser window) to download and install the game.

To experience *Fortnite: Battle Royale* on an Xbox One, you must have a paid Xbox Live Gold account. The PS4 version of the game is available from the Playstation Network, while the Nintendo Switch version can be downloaded from the Nintendo eShop.

Users of iPhone and iPad devices should download the free *Fortnite* app from the App Store, while Android-based mobile device users will find a link to the Fortnite mobile app at Fortnite.com.

Regardless of which gaming platform you use, you'll need to set up a free Epic Games account to play *Fortnite: Battle Royale*, although in some cases, you're able to establish a game account using your existing account information related to your gaming system's online service. To create or manage your Epic Games account, visit: https://accounts.epicgames.com /register/customized.

What You Need to Know About Battle Passes

In conjunction with the launch of each new *Fortnite: Battle Royale* season, Epic Games kicks off a new Battle Pass. These are divided into a series of tier-based challenges. Each time you complete a specific challenge or complete the group of challenges posed within a tier, you'll unlock items that can be used to customize your character. Other items, such as bonus XP, XP multipliers, and 100 V-Buck bundles, are also sometimes offered as a prize for completing challenges.

During game play, you have the ability to earn experience points (XP) by accomplishing certain tasks. These tasks might include defeating an enemy or completing specific in-game objectives (like dealing damage with a specific type of weapon or opening a specific number of chests within a particular point of interest). Earning experience points helps you boost your player level, and often helps you achieve certain Free Pass and Battle Pass–related challenges.

Everyone can participate in the Free Pass challenges for free (without purchasing a Battle Pass), but the items and prizes that can be unlocked by completing these challenges are not as rare or exciting as the ones offered to gamers who have completed Battle Pass-related challenges.

During each season, a Battle Pass can be purchased for 950 V-Bucks (slightly less than $10 US). It's best to purchase it right at the start of a new season, but it can be purchased anytime. Every three months or so, when a new gaming season begins, a new Battle Pass (offering new challenges) can be purchased, and the old one will expire.

As a bonus, the Season 5 Battle Pass included several free outfits. This Battle Pass included 100 tiers, with 100 rewards that could ultimately be unlocked.

If you opt to purchase a Battle Pass, you have two choices. You can purchase just the Battle Pass or purchase the Battle Pass with 25 tiers unlocked (meaning that you automatically and immediately receive the prizes associated with those 25 tiers without having to complete the related challenges).

To initially purchase a Battle Pass (after acquiring V-Bucks), from the Lobby, access the Battle Pass screen. In the lower-left corner of the screen, you'll see the Purchase option. Press the appropriate controller or keyboard button to make the purchase. The current price of the Battle Pass is displayed. Select your option and confirm your purchase decision.

Upon confirming your purchase, the current Battle Pass will immediately be activated.

If you've acquired the package that unlocks 25 tiers for 2,800 V-Bucks, those tier-related prizes are awarded to you immediately and unlocked within the game. Items that are unlocked get stored in the Locker. XP bonuses, XP Multipliers, or V-Buck bundles will be added to your account.

The Season 5 Battle Pass included several new outfits, along with a bunch of other goodies.

Either from the left side of the Lobby screen, or by selecting the Challenges tab from the Lobby, view the current challenges, so you know what needs to be accomplished when playing *Fortnite: Battle Royale* moving forward.

How to Purchase Battle Pass Tiers

If a particular series of Battle Pass tier-related challenges is too difficult or time consuming, for 150 V-Bucks each, you're able to immediately unlock one tier at a time and receive those prizes. To do this, from the Lobby, return to the Battle Pass screen. In the lower-left corner, you'll see the Purchase Tier button. This only applies if you have already purchased the current Battle Pass.

Select the Purchase Tier option.

Confirm your purchase decision by pressing the appropriate controller button or keyboard key. The prize(s) associated with that tier will immediately be unlocked.

One of the great things about accomplishing daily, weekly, Free Pass, and Battle Pass tier-related challenges is that they don't just focus on defeating enemies and winning matches. These challenges encourage you to accomplish other tasks within the game that often involve exploration, harvesting and collecting resources, finding and using specific loot items, or using a specific type of weapon.

Customize Options from the Settings Menu

If you're new to playing *Fortnite: Battle Royale*, consider leaving most of the adjustable game options available from the Settings menu at their default settings. Later, as you get more acquainted with the game and develop your skills, you might choose to tweak some of these settings.

Often, expert *Fortnite: Battle Royale* gamers reveal their personalized game settings as part of their Twitch.tv live streams or YouTube videos. Don't just copy the settings of an expert gamer. If you're using a different gaming platform, it'll react differently. Meanwhile, if you're not as good a player, adjusting the settings the wrong way could actually make you an even worse player. As you keep practicing, tweak the various settings in ways that make the most sense for you personally, based on the strategies you typically use when playing.

To access the Settings menu, first access the game's Menu. The icon for it is displayed in the top-right corner of the Lobby screen. It looks like three horizontal lines. To access this menu, you'll need to press the Options button on the PS4 controller, or the "+" button on the Nintendo Switch controller, for example. Whenever there's an important announcement from Epic Games, it'll be displayed near the bottom-center of the Lobby screen. Here, an announcement about a pending game update is displayed.

Open the menu that's displayed near the top-right corner of the screen and select the gear-shaped Settings menu icon. A selection of submenus, starting with the Game Settings submenu is displayed. One at a time, scroll through the menus and make the feature adjustments you deem necessary.

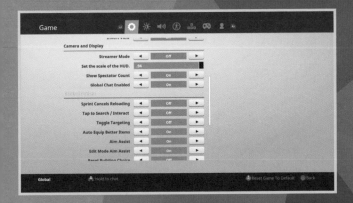

From the Game Settings menu, new *Fortnite: Battle Royale* players should make sure features like Auto Equip Better Items, Aim Assist, Edit Mode Aim Assist, Turbo Building, Auto Material Change, and Controller Auto-Run are all turned on.

Controller Layout Options

If you're using a controller on your Xbox One, PS4, or Nintendo Switch, for example, you're able to choose between several controller configurations from the Controller menu. Options include: Old School, Quick Builder, Combat Pro, or Builder Pro.

Choose whichever controller layout best fits your personal gaming style, and then memorize what each button does, so you can access the right command or function quickly during the game.

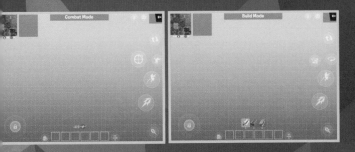

Mobile device users can choose between Combat mode or Build mode, and then

customize the on-screen icons and buttons using this HUD Layout Tool, which is accessible when you access the Menu option from the Lobby.

PC and Mac gamers can either use their mouse and keyboard to control the game or take advantage of an optional game controller. When using the mouse and keyboard, you're able to assign specific game functions to specific keyboard keys or mouse buttons in order to further customize your game play experience.

A Gaming Headset Is Highly Recommended!

Sound effects play an extremely important role in *Fortnite: Battle Royale*, and it's essential that you're always able to clearly hear the sound effects. For example, you can often hear the footsteps of an enemy soldier approaching, before they actually come into view.

You'll hear the opening and closing of doors within structures, as well as the sounds of enemies using their pickaxes to smash things. As soldiers build, this too makes sounds that can reveal their locations. You'll also hear the unique sound chests generate. This will help you locate them if they're above or below you or hidden behind a wall or object. Meanwhile, the sounds generated by the storm will alert you when it's about to expand and potentially engulf you.

Audio									

Music Volume	0.35	
Sound FX Volume	0.82	Adjust the volume of fx sound.
Dialog Volume	0.47	
Voice Chat Volume	0.62	
Cinematics Volume	0.50	
Subtitles	◄ On ►	
Voice Chat	◄ On ►	

Global   🎮 Hold to chat   △ Apply   ☐ Restore   ○ Back

At the very least, play this game while wearing stereo headphones, and from the Sound Settings menu within the game, consider turning down the Music option, and turning up the Sound FX option. If you'll be playing with teammates and have a gaming headset with a built-in microphone, also turn up the Voice Chat Volume option, so you can hear everything your teammates say, even when bullets are flying and explosions are happening all around you.

Especially if you'll be playing Duo or Squads mode (or any team-oriented game play mode), using a gaming headset when experiencing a match is highly recommended. Not only will you be able to hear the in-game sound effects the way they were meant to be heard, but you'll be able to speak in real-time with your allies and teammates during each match.

Turtle Beach Corp. (www.turtlebeach.com) is just one of many companies that offer high-quality gaming headsets with a built-in microphone. The wired Stealth 600 version comes with a 3.5mm headphone jack or USB connector that plugs into a computer, gaming console, or mobile device. The wireless Stealth 700 version uses Bluetooth to connect to the gaming system you're using. Plan on spending between $99.00 and $200.00 for a top-quality gaming headset, regardless of the manufacturer.

Fortnite: Battle Royale Offers Cross-Platform Compatibility

Epic Games has made Fortnite: Battle Royale cross-platform compatible, which means it does not matter which gaming platform you or your teammates are using. You can still participate in the same matches and compete against other gamers using any compatible gaming platform. For this functionality to work, the in-game settings must be adjusted correctly.

That being said, Sony has purposely made the PS4 edition of Fortnite: Battle Royale incompatible with the Nintendo Switch version. As a result, if you have both of these systems, you can't use the same account to go back and forth and play on whichever system you want. Two separate game accounts will be required. You also can't play with or compete against players on a PS4 if you're using a Nintendo Switch (or vice versa). Hopefully this will change in the future.

CHAPTER 2

HOW TO CUSTOMIZE
YOUR CHARACTER'S APPEARANCE

One feature that gamers love in *Fortnite: Battle Royale* is the ability to customize the appearance of their soldier. This can be done by purchasing, unlocking, or acquiring individual items.

To purchase V-Bucks, access the Shop from the Lobby. You can then choose a V-Bucks pack to purchase for between $4.99 (US) and $99.99 (US). The more V-Bucks you purchase at once, the cheaper they become.

Choosing an Outfit

Outfits are the clothes worn by your character. Every day within the Item Shop, several new outfits are released by Epic Games. The outfits offered as Featured Items tend to be rare or limited edition, and only available for a short time. Before each match, you're able to alter the appearance of your soldier, if you've acquired optional items.

Individual outfits sold by the Item Shop cost between 800 and 2,000 V-bucks each. (This translates to between approximately $8.00 US and $20.00 US.)

Here, the Fourth of July–themed Fireworks Team Leader outfit (which was available for a very limited time) is about to be purchased for 1,500 V-Bucks (approximately $15 US). It includes a related back bling design. All items you purchase, unlock, or acquire are yours to keep and use forever. They do not expire. You'll find your items within the Locker. From the Locker, you're able to choose which items you want to apply to your soldier. Only items you've purchased, unlocked, or acquired are available to you.

If you often play with the same group of squad members, consider selecting the same or similar outfits (so you all match and look like a team), and then have each person customize their soldier's appearance with a different back bling design and/or pickaxe design.

When all four players in a squad look the same and are clearly working together, they're instantly identified as a squad by everyone else participating in the match. You can use this to your advantage to intimidate opponents. However, it could also attract extra attention from competing squads, and make your squad their primary target until you're defeated (or you defeat them).

It's common for highly skilled *Fortnite: Battle Royale* players to wear the more "epic," rare, limited-edition, or unusual outfits, complete with the matching pickaxe, glider, and back bling designs. As a result, other players in the game assume enemies wearing these outfits are being controlled by the top-notch players. To confuse your opponents, especially when you become highly skilled, consider sticking with the default (and free) outfit worn by noobs (beginners). The other players won't expect you to be a threat.

Check out this sample collection of previously released and popular outfits. Some are occasionally re-released in the Items Shop.

With its Asian theme, this Wukong outfit is considered "legendary" and ultra-rare.

The Cuddle Team Leader outfit is also "legendary" and rare, but it has a more whimsical appearance. Do you have the light-hearted and bubbly personality to rock it during a match?

If you have a sweet tooth and enjoy candy, you'll love this Zoey outfit, which has a bright-colored candy theme.

At the same time Epic Games introduced the spray paint emotes into the game, this "Epic" Abstrakt outfit was released.

The "legendary" Raven outfit is both sinister and mysterious looking. It's bound to strike fear into enemies you encounter when your soldier wears it.

Venturion is one of the slick-looking, more futuristic outfits that was made available for a limited time. It became an instant classic.

Who doesn't love pizza? Share your pizza passion by choosing the Tomatohead outfit. It's offered periodically for sale from the Item Shop. Add the optional pizza delivery box themed back bling and the pizza cutter pickaxe design (sold separately), and you'll complete the look. Don't worry, you won't appear too cheesy wearing this optional outfit.

Occasionally, themed outfits are released based on the storyline that's unfolding within the game, or that correspond to a special event or holiday happening in the real world. Typically, outfits are sold separately from related pickaxe designs, but once in a while Epic Games offers bundles that include multiple items. This Noir outfit was originally released near the end of Season 4. It was part of the "Hardboiled Set," which was priced at 1,500 V-Bucks. It included the outfit, related back bling, and related pickaxe design.

This "Epic" Huntress outfit has a Viking theme and is part of the Norse set. It was one of the first outfits to be released at the start of Season 5.

Check out this "Legendary" Drift outfit, which was also among the first to be introduced at the start of Season 5.

Add Optional Back Bling to Your Character's Outfit

Typically, in conjunction with each outfit, a matching backpack design (back bling) is offered. Keep in mind, you can mix and match outfits with back bling, glider designs, and pickaxe designs from other sets to give your soldier an even more unique appearance.

Once you purchase, unlock, or acquire a back bling item, it becomes available from the Locker. When viewing the Locker screen, select the Back Bling slot to see the selection of back bling designs you own and that are available to you, and then choose one to apply to your character.

Choose a Glider Design

The glider is used when your soldier jumps from the Battle Bus at the start of a match and is activated to ensure a safe landing. During a match, a glider is also used when you take advantage of a Launch Pad or travel through a rift. While many different glider designs are available, all gliders function exactly the same way. None offers an advantage when used within the game.

Select a Pickaxe Design

At the start of a match, when your soldier lands on the island, he or she is armed only with their pickaxe. By purchasing, unlocking, or acquiring additional pickaxe designs, you can customize the appearance of this resource harvesting tool (which can also be a close combat weapon).

The pickaxe is seen and used often during a match. Regardless of which pickaxe design you select, they all function exactly the same way. In any house, for example, use the pickaxe to smash metal appliances in the kitchen to harvest metal. (Shown here on an iPad Pro.)

If you need help coming up with an awesome combination of items for your soldier to wear and use, select this randomize option, and let the game decide which item to select.

Contrail Designs

Once your soldier leaps from the Battle Bus he or she begins their freefall toward land. If you've unlocked a contrail design, this is the animated graphic you'll see trailing behind them during their decent.

Contrail designs typically need to be unlocked by completing challenges. They're rarely, if ever, offered for sale from the Item Shop. They may, however, be offered as a free download as part of a free Twitch Prime Pack, for example, which is periodically offered to Amazon Prime subscribers who also have a free Twitch.tv account. Visit www.twitch.tv/prime/fortnite for more info.

Communicate Using Emotes

While you're visiting the pre-deployment area, or anytime during a match, one way to communicate with all other gamers in the same area as your soldier is to use an emote. *Fortnite: Battle Royale* offers several types of emotes, each of which must be purchased, unlocked, or acquired separately.

Dance Moves—Many different dance moves are available. They can be used separately, or you can create your own choreography by using several different dance moves back-to-back (in quick succession). Gamers often use dance moves as a greeting in the pre-deployment area, but during a match, they're often used to gloat about a victory or to taunt enemies.

Graphic Emotes—A large collection of individual graphic icons can be acquired and used. When one is selected, your soldier will toss it into the air for everyone around to see. The icon disappears after a few seconds.

Spray Paint Tags—Armed with a virtual spray paint can, your soldier can paint on any flat surface on the island, such as the ground or the side of a building. Many different spray paint tag designs are available separately.

Use one spray paint tag at a time, or mix and match two or more of them to create interesting-looking graffiti on the island. Anytime you take time to use an emote, make sure it's safe to do so. You can't use a weapon at the same time you're using an emote, so you'll be vulnerable to attack during a match.

How to Acquire and Use Emotes

Each day, different dance moves, graphic emotes, and spray paint tag emotes are sold separately from the Item Shop. They typically cost between 500 and 800 V-Bucks each. They can also be unlocked by completing certain challenges or acquired as part of a Twitch Prime Pack.

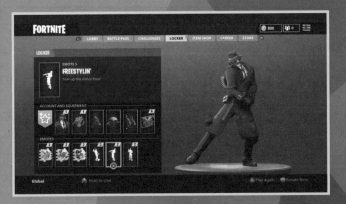

Before a match, equip your soldier with up to six different emotes. To do this, visit the Locker. Below the Emotes heading on the left side of the screen, you'll see six slots. Select and open one slot at a time.

Whenever you're in the pre-deployment area before a match, or during any match, to use an emote, press the Emotes button on your controller or keyboard, and from the pop-up Emotes menu that's displayed on the screen, choose the emote you want to use.

Once you've selected an available slot, a listing of emotes that are available to you is displayed. This will include all of the dance moves, as well as the graphic emotes and spray paint tag designs available to you. When you select an emote that's displayed on the left side of the screen, a preview of it is showcased on the right side of the screen. Use the Save and Exit option to choose the selected emote for the slot that's active. Do this for each available emote slot, assuming you've acquired a collection of at least six different emotes.

One way to use a dance move when you're playing a Duos or Squads match, for example, is to have one team member hide and prepare to launch a surprise attack on an enemy. Have another team member go out in the open and start dancing to attract attention. As soon as the enemy soldier reveals himself and tries to attack the dancer, his or her team member(s) can launch their attack on the enemies.

Once you defeat an enemy, assuming it's safe to do so, use a dance move to brag about your victory. The gamer you just defeated will likely see it from Spectator mode, before he or she returns to the Lobby after being eliminated from the match.

EARLY ACCESS

LOADING...

Only YOU can prevent V-Buck Scams
Do not share your password with anyone.

Anytime you purchase V-Bucks, this requires using real money. You'll also need to use your Epic Games, Playstation Network, Xbox Live Gold, or App Store account, for example, to make the purchase. Always protect your account information, and never give out your account password to anyone, especially when you're talking with other gamers while playing one of *Fortnite: Battle Royale*'s team-oriented modes.

Watch What You Say!

Anytime you play one of *Fortnite: Battle Royale*'s team-oriented game play modes and use the Fill option, you'll potentially be playing with strangers. When using a gaming headset, you're able to talk with these people. Be careful what you say and what personal information you share with these people. Remember, they're strangers! Never give out your last name, phone number, address, or other details (like what school you go to).

CHAPTER 3
YOUR ISLAND ADVENTURE IS ABOUT TO BEGIN

Whether it's a result of comets, missiles, other virtual disasters, or other inspirations, Epic Games continues to use the game's storyline to introduce new points of interest to the island, make drastic changes to older locations, and periodically remove established sites from the island altogether. Each change provides new terrain to explore, and potential new obstacles to overcome.

At the start of Season 5, Moisty Mire was replaced by Paradise Palms, while Anarchy Acres was replaced by Lazy Lanes. The soccer stadium that was located near Junk Junction was removed, but many small (unlabeled) points of interest were added to the map. Several familiar points of

interest, like Dusty Divot, were given a makeover. Tomato Town was also redesigned and renamed to Tomato Temple toward the end of Season 5.

This is what the island map looked like near the end of Season 5.

At the start of Season 5, the island evolved with the introduction of new points of interest, plus all-new desert terrain.

The better you get to know the island, including where points of interest are located, and what you can expect within each location (including the type of terrain each offers), the easier it'll be to create successful strategies and equip your backpack with the best weapons and loot items to help you survive when visiting each location.

As you're exploring, if you walk into a rift, you'll be transported. Use this as an emergency escape if you're being attacked, or if you just want to explore a different area of the island. You can also use a Rift-to-Go loot item to transport your soldier to another location quickly.

Continuously displayed on the screen during a match is the Location Map. It shows a small area of the island around your current location. Depending on which gaming platform you're using, it'll be located in the top-right or top-left corner of the screen. The white triangle displayed on this map is your current location. Colored triangle icons represent team members who are nearby. You can't see the location of enemies on the map.

Once airborne, use your directional controls to navigate, and use the glider to ensure a safe landing. Get ready to explore!

You Can Learn a Lot from the Island Maps

There are several versions of the island map you need to become acquainted with.

On the Location Map, areas in pink have already been engulfed by the storm. If you see a white line on the map, this is the path to follow to reach safety when the storm is expanding and approaching your location.

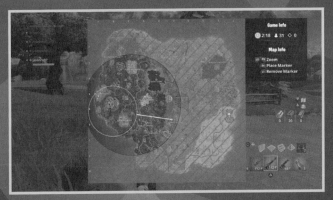

When you see a portion of the circle on the Location Map, this represents the border between the unsafe storm ravaged area and the safe area of the island, based on your current location.

Checking the island map during a match reveals a lot of useful information.

Here's what you can learn from the island map during a match:

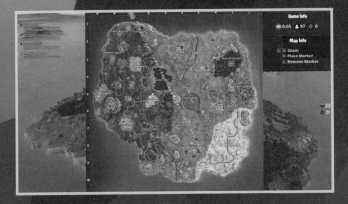

During the time you're in the pre-deployment area waiting to board the Battle Bus, or for the first 20 seconds or so that you're riding the bus, access the large island map to see the random route the Battle Bus will be taking over the island. Knowing this can help you and your team choose your landing location. Use Place Markers to display location flares for your allies. The buttons to press to set a Place Marker are listed in the top-right corner of the screen.

- The random route the Battle Bus will take across the island as it drops you off. This route is only displayed while you're in the pre-deployment area and for the first few seconds while aboard the Battle Bus.
- The location of each point of interest on the island.
- Your current location.
- The location of your teammate(s) if you're experiencing the Duos or Squads game play modes, for example.
- The current location of the storm.
- Where the storm will be expanding and moving to next.

Especially if you're playing *Fortnite: Battle Royale* on a 4K resolution television set or high-definition computer monitor, whenever you look at the map in Season 5 or beyond, you'll see much more detail than ever before.

Each time the storm is about to expand and move, you'll hear a ticking sound effect, and a warning message appears in the center of the screen. Check the timer (displayed below the Location Map) to determine when the storm will be expanding next.

Learn How Map Coordinates Work

Whenever you look at the large island map, you'll discover it's divided into quadrants. Along the top of the map are the letters "A" through "J." Along the left edge of the map are the numbers "1" through "10." Each point of interest or location on the map can be found by its unique coordinates.

For example, Tilted Towers can be found at map coordinates D5.5, and Snobby Shores is located at coordinates A5. At the start of Season 5, Paradise Palms replaced Moisty Mire and was centered around map coordinates I8, while Anarchy Acres was replaced by Lazy Links at map coordinates F2.5.

As you're looking at the island map, you're able to zoom in on specific areas to get a better look. In future versions of the game, Epic Games has said that the resolution of the map, especially when you zoom in, will improve greatly. Here, you're looking at map coordinates I9.5, which is part of Paradise Palms. As you can see from the red, yellow, white, and blue colored triangles, all four squad members are congregated here. In just under two minutes, the storm will move and expand. Based on the white line that shows the route to follow to avoid the storm, this squad has a hike ahead of them to remain safe. Finding an ATK vehicle would speed up the journey a lot.

Options for Choosing Your Partner or Squad Members

As you know, *Fortnite: Battle Royale* offers three permanent game play modes—Solo, Duos, and Squads. At least one or two additional, but temporary game play modes are also offered at any given time.

Choose your desired game play mode from the Lobby prior to a match. The selected game play mode is displayed on the lower-right side of the Lobby screen, directly above the Play option. Here, Squads mode (with the Don't Fill option) is selected.

From the Lobby, press the appropriate controller button or keyboard mouse button, based on which gaming platform you're using, to access the Choose Game Mode screen.

Take Advantage of the Game's Fill Feature

If you highlight and select the Duos or Squads option, for example, just above the Accept banner, you'll see an option that says Fill or Don't Fill, along with the controller button or mouse/keyboard key to toggle between these two options. Here, the Fill option is selected.

Anytime you plan to invite people you know to be your teammate in Duos mode (or your squad mates in Squads mode), choose the **Don't Fill** option. However, if you want the game to automatically match you up with a partner or squad mates, make sure the **Fill** option is selected.

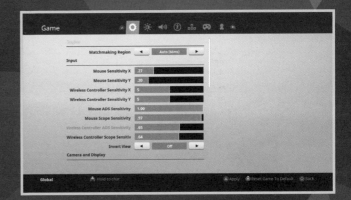

Who you get teamed up with when using the Fill feature will depend on how you've adjusted your game settings, and which regional game server you're connected to. To adjust this, access the Game Settings menu, and change the option for the Matchmaking Region option (displayed at the top of the menu). For the fastest response time, choose Auto. If you select a specific region, such as NA-East (North America-East Coast), NA-West (North America-West Coast), Europe, Oceania, Brazil, or Asia, the response time may be slower. If you want to play with specific people, you all should be logged into the same region's server.

How to Invite Your Online Friends Using the Party Finder

If you're playing *Fortnite: Battle Royale* on a Playstation 4, you must be active on Sony's online-based Playstation Network to experience the game.

Through the Playstation Network, you can make online friends, and then invite those people to play *Fortnite: Battle Royale* with you. To learn more about this feature, visit: www.playstation.com/en-us/explore/ps4/features/#connect.

Xbox One gamers need to have a paid membership to Xbox Live Gold (www.xbox.com/en-US/live). This service also allows you to make online friends, and then invite those friends to play *Fortnite: Battle Royale* with you.

Nintendo Switch players have the option to join Nintendo Switch Online (www.nintendo.com/switch/online-service) which launched in September 2018. It also allows gamers to make online friends and challenge them in compatible games.

It's important to link up your Playstation Network, Xbox Live Gold, or Nintendo account with your Epic Games account in order to play *Fortnite: Battle Royale* with your online friends from these services. The linking process only needs to be done once.

For step-by-step directions for linking your accounts, visit the appropriate webpage:

Playstation 4—https://fortnitehelp.epicgames.com/customer/en/portal/articles/2845438-how-do-i-connect-my-psn-account-to-my-epic-account

XboxOne—https://fortnitehelp.epicgames.com/customer/en/portal/articles/2843279-how-do-i-connect-my-xbox-account-to-my-epic-account

Nintendo Switch—https://fortnitehelp.epicgames.com/customer/en/portal/articles/2943456-how-do-i-connect-my-nintendo-account-to-my-epic-account

Make Some Epic Friends

The easiest way to find and make friends to experience *Fortnite: Battle Royale* with is to create and use your free Epic Games account (https://accounts.epicgames.com/login). Anytime you add squad members prior to a match, this is referred to as "squading up."

From the Lobby screen, access the game menu using the appropriate button on your controller or keyboard/mouse.

Select the Epic Friends option to see the online status of existing Epic Friends, find and add new Epic Friends, and manage Settings related to your friends. These options are displayed below the Manage Epic Friends heading, found near the top-right corner of the screen.

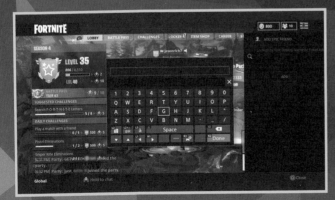

Highlight the Add Friends icon (which looks like a head and a plus sign). Within the Search

field, enter someone's Epic Display Name or their email address to find and add them.

To see an existing friend's online status, select the Status icon, and then scroll down your friends' list to highlight someone's name. If they're online and available, a green dot appears to the left of their username. A red dot means that person is not online or available to play.

Access the communications menu associated with the selected friend to send them a message (Whisper), join their party, invite them to join your party, remove that person from your friends list, or block that gamer. This can be seen on the right side of the screen.

To add Epic Friends to your team or squad, from the Lobby, highlight and select one of the "+" symbols, and select the Party Finder option.

From the Party Finder window, scroll through your listing of Epic Friends.

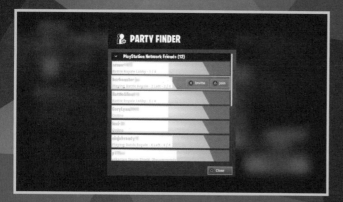

Each time a gamer is highlighted, an Invite and Join option is displayed to the right of their username. Based on the text displayed below their username, you can easily see if that person is currently available, playing *Fortnite: Battle Royale*, or if they too are hanging out in the Lobby looking for people to play with. Press the appropriate Invite or Join option, based on whether you want to invite someone to your team or squad, or if you want to join someone else's team or squad prior to a match beginning.

Once a Duos or Squad match begins, you and your teammates will be transported to the pre-deployment area. Now is the time when you want to study the appearance of your teammates, so you can easily identify them on the island, based on their outfit and username. If each of you are using a gaming headset (with a microphone), you'll be able to speak with your teammates. Use this time in the pre-deployment area and then on the Battle Bus to choose your landing location and start planning your strategy.

Choose the Perfect Landing Location

When you land within a popular point of interest, like Tilted Towers, you'll almost definitely encounter enemy soldiers within seconds. Upon landing, take cover and quickly find and grab a weapon, so you'll be able to fight. Otherwise, you'll often be shot and defeated almost immediately upon landing.

You can count on having to engage in firefights when visiting the more popular points of interest. Instead of landing directly in one of these places, consider landing in the outskirts. This is a view from outside of Tilted Tower. Collect weapons, ammo, and/or loot items from surrounding structures and areas, and then enter into the point of interest on foot when you're better armed and prepared to fight.

If you land in a popular area and immediately encounter other soldiers, consider rushing them with your pickaxe and launching an attack. When your squad mates are nearby, have multiple people team up against one enemy for a quicker victory.

Using only the pickaxe, you'll need to make several direct hits to defeat an enemy. Keep jumping around and moving in between

pickaxe swings to avoid getting hit by the opponent's pickaxe attacks. However, if the adversary landed a few seconds before you and managed to grab a nearby weapon, run away before you get shot. Here, the soldier holding the pickaxe was too slow for the enemy armed with a weapon.

How to Set and Identify Place Markers

While in the pre-deployment area or while on the Battle Bus, access the island map and place a marker where you've chosen to land. Once you and your teammates place a marker and then exit the Battle Bus, you'll see a colored flare as you fall. Each colored flare represents one of your teammates. Check the top-left corner of the screen to see which color corresponds with each team member.

You can also use map markers to help regroup at any time during a match.

During freefall and once the glider is activated, follow the colored flares (which only your teammates can see) and use the directional controls, so you all land at the same location.

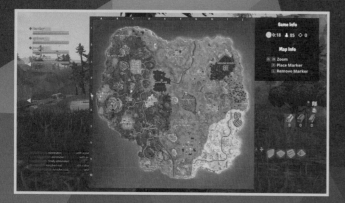

Once everyone lands on the island, check the island map to keep tabs of everyone's location. During this match, the four squad members separated. One person headed to Flush Factory, two were traveling together between points of interest (near map coordinates C5), and the fourth decided to fend for himself in Salty Springs.

Sticking together during a match is often useful, but don't stay very close together, unless you have to. When multiple team members are standing in close proximity, this makes them an easy target for enemies, and multiple team members could get injured at once.

If you're playing with teammates selected by the game using the Fill option, not all of your team members will always know how to mark their intended landing location on the island map. If players aren't using a gaming headset, it's difficult to discuss a designated landing spot. In this case, keep an eye on the map when the Battle Bus is flying over the island, and watch for the colored triangle markers that represent the location of your teammates to appear on the island map once the allied soldiers leap from the bus. Follow them to where they land, so the team can stick together.

Help Keep Your Teammates Alive

Anytime you play Solo mode, if an enemy defeats you in combat, you'll immediately be eliminated from the match. However, when playing Duos or Squads, for example, if you or one of your teammates gets attacked, there's a short window when the injured soldier can be revived by someone else.

At any time, one squad member can open his or her Backpack Inventory screen and drop an item they're holding. This allows one of their nearby teammates to pick it up and use it. This can be done with weapons, ammo, loot items, or resources. Here Bandages are about to be shared.

When one teammate has been badly wounded, they'll fall to the ground and be unable to do anything but very slowly crawl around.

Once a soldier is wounded, two things can happen. An enemy can approach and finish off the wounded soldier, or one of the wounded soldier's teammates can revive him. To revive a teammate, walk up to him or her and press the Revive button on the controller/keyboard.

Here, the fallen soldier is being revived by a teammate. You can see the injured soldier's Health meter increasing as the Revive timer (the circular timer near the bottom-center of the screen) ticks away. By looking at the top-left corner of the screen, you can see that one team member has been eliminated from the match, one is badly injured, and two have almost full Health.

How to Revive Wounded Teammates

Teamwork when playing the Duos or Squads game play mode is essential. If one of your teammates gets injured, other team members can revive them before the injured soldier is eliminated from the match altogether. As always, work quickly, and be on the lookout for nearby enemies!

When a solider is wounded, their Health meter turns red and slowly gets depleted. That soldier must be revived before this happens, or before an enemy soldier finishes them off. Here, an enemy soldier is about to finish off the wounded soldier with one final shot. The injured soldier's teammates didn't reach him in time to offer assistance.

Follow these steps to revive a wounded teammate:

1. You can discover a teammate has been wounded by checking their Health meter in the top-left corner of the screen. A red "+" will also appear next to the team member's name on the main game screen. Plus, the injured team member can use the Quick Chat menu's Need Meds option. If all players are using gaming headsets, the injured soldier can simply ask for help and share their location.
2. To protect yourself and your teammate, build a protective wall around you both. This is optional but recommended in case enemies are still close by. Within the four surrounding walls, build a ramp/staircase, and hide under that. Then build a roof on top of the structure. Ideally, you want to use stone

or metal when building a defensive fortress, so it can withstand more powerful incoming attacks.

3. While one teammate revives another, when playing in Squads mode, two other teammates can stand guard and, if necessary, fight off enemies.
4. The healthy soldier should walk directly up to their injured teammate. Press the Revive button on your controller (or keyboard/mouse) to begin the revival process which will take at least 10 seconds, during which time both soldiers are vulnerable to enemy attack.
5. The healthy soldier can then drop an HP power-up loot item (such as a Med Kit, Bandages, or a Chug Jug), which the injured soldier can pick up and immediately use in order to regain additional Health before rejoining the match.

When one of your squad members is injured, get close to them and press the Revive button to bring them back to health.

Learn to Speak *Fortnite*: Practice Communicating with Your Teammates

When all of your teammates are using gaming headsets and can talk during a match, this makes it much easier to plan and execute successful strategies. Because the action is so fast-paced, however, you'll seldom have time to hold long, drawn out conversations. Instead, learn to communicate quickly and succinctly, so you can get your message across while focusing on the action that's happening on the screen.

Displayed at the top-center of the screen are compass directions that are displayed in real-time. By glancing at this compass, you can quickly tell your teammates from what direction enemies are approaching, or where to look to see an enemy that's hiding. For example, you could say, "Enemy Fort, straight ahead, West" or "Sniper, upwards, North at 15 degrees."

When trying to describe the location of something, don't just blurt out, "In front of me" or "Behind me." This information is not useful unless your teammates are next to you and facing the same direction.

CHAPTER 4
FINDING, COLLECTING, SHARING, AND USING WEAPONS

Available throughout the island are hundreds of different types of weapons. The trick is to find and collect the best weapons (and related ammunition) that'll help you survive and defeat your enemies.

The weapon categories these firearms and explosives typically fall into include: Assault Rifles, Grenade Launchers, Grenades, Miniguns, Pistols, Rocket Launchers, Shotguns, SMGs (Sub Machine Guns), and Sniper Rifles. Other types of weapons are always being introduced into the game.

Many *Fortnite* gamers agree that the most useful weapon to master using is any type of shotgun. There are many types to choose from, and shotguns are more powerful than a pistol. When viewing the Backpack Inventory screen, details about the selected weapon/item you're holding are displayed. Here, details about the Pump Shotgun are displayed.

Shotguns can be used in close-range or mid-range combat situations, or even at a distance. (From a distance, they're harder to aim accurately than a rifle with a scope, for example.) When using a shotgun, always try for a headshot to inflict the most damage.

Each category of weapon can be used for a different purpose. Based on the type of enemy encounter you're experiencing at any given moment, it's essential that you choose the most appropriate and powerful weapon at your disposal.

Before engaging in a firefight, consider:

- The selection of weapons currently in your backpack and available to you.

- The amount of ammo you currently have for each weapon. (Be sure to pick up as much ammo as you can throughout each match.)
- The distance you are from your opponent.
- Your surroundings, and whether or not your weapon will need to destroy a barrier, fortress wall, or shielding before it can inflict damage on an enemy.
- Your own skill level as a gamer, and your speed when it comes to selecting, targeting/aiming, and then firing your weapon.
- How much backup you can expect from your teammates. Anytime two or more of your teammates work together against a single enemy soldier, you'll be at an advantage, especially if your team can attack the enemy from multiple sides simultaneously.

In each weapon category, up to a dozen or more different types of weapons may become accessible to you. Epic Games regularly tweaks the selection of weapons available, as well as the capabilities of each weapon.

Three Tips to Improve Your Shooting Accuracy

Regardless of which weapon you're using, your aim improves when you crouch down

and you press the Aim button for the weapon you're using. When you press the Aim button before the trigger button, you'll zoom in a bit on your opponent, and you'll have more precise control over the positioning of the targeting crosshairs.

While it's often necessary to be running or jumping at the same time you're firing a weapon your accuracy improves when you're standing still. It improves even more when you press the Aim button before pressing the trigger button.

You almost always have an advantage when you're higher up than your opponent and shooting in a downward direction. On the left is the view from above when using the scope of a rifle. You can really zoom in on an enemy who's lower than you and far away.

On the right, the soldier is in the same position, but he switched from a sniper rifle to a gun without a scope. He still gains a tactical height advantage by shooting enemies from above.

Understand How Weapons Are Rated and Categorized

While every weapon has the ability to cause damage and defeat your adversaries, each is rated based on several criteria, including its rarity. Weapons are color-coded with a hue around them to showcase their rarity.

Weapons with a **purple** hue are "Epic."

Weapons with a **gray** hue are "Common."

Weapon with a **green** hue are "Uncommon."

"Legendary" weapons (with an **orange** hue) are hard to find, extra powerful, and very rare. If you're able to obtain one, grab it!

It is possible to collect several of the same weapon, but each could have a different rarity. So, if you collect two of the same weapon, and one is rare, but the second is legendary, definitely keep the legendary weapon and trade the other for something else when you find a replacement.

When there's a powerful weapon you've collected, but no longer have a need for, offer it to one of your teammates before dropping it at a random location where it can potentially be picked up and used by an enemy.

Weapons with a **blue** hue are "Rare."

To drop a weapon for your teammate to pick up, get close to the teammate you want to share with. Then, from your Backpack Inventory screen, select the weapon you want to give away, and press the Drop button on the controller (or mouse/keyboard). Your teammate can now pick up that weapon. This also works for ammunition, loot items, and resources. Sharing weapons (and ammo) is one way you can ensure everyone on your team is well armed before a firefight, so while you're confronting enemies, you can work together to achieve victory. Here, one soldier is about to give his squad mate a revolver by dropping it in front of him.

DPS Rating—This stands for "Damage Per Second." Use this rating to help estimate a weapon's power. It does not take into account things like accuracy of your aim, or the extra damage you can inflict by making a headshot, for example. In general, DPS is calculated by multiplying the damage the weapon can cause by its fire rate.

The rarity of a weapon contributes heavily to its Damage Per Second (DPS) Rating. Thus, the DPS Rating for a legendary weapon is much higher than the DPS Rating for an identical weapon that has a common rarity, for example.

Damage Rating—A numeric rating, based on how much potential damage a weapon can cause per direct hit.

Fire Rate—This refers to the number of bullets fired per second. Some of the most powerful weapons have a slow fire rate, so to inflict the most damage, your aim needs to be perfect. Otherwise, during the time the weapon takes in between shots, your enemy could move, or launch their own counter attack.

MAG (Magazine) Capacity—This is the total number of ammunition rounds (or bullets) the weapon can fire before it needs to be reloaded. Reloading a weapon takes valuable time, during which your soldier will be vulnerable to attack. Your enemy could also move, meaning you'll need to re-aim your weapon. Switching weapons is often faster than waiting for a slow weapon to reload.

Reload Time—The number of seconds it takes to reload the weapon, assuming you have replacement ammo available. Some of the most powerful weapons have a very slow reload time, so if your shooting accuracy isn't great, you'll be at a disadvantage.

There are plenty of websites, including: IGN.com (www.ign.com/wikis/fortnite/Weapons), Gameskinny.com (www.gameskinny.com/9mt22/complete-fortnite-battle-royale-weapons-stats-list), and RankedBoost.com (https://rankedboost.com/fortnite/best-weapons-tier-list), that provide the current stats for each weapon offered in *Fortnite: Battle Royale*, based on the latest tweaks made to the game. Just make sure when you look at this information online, it refers to the most recently released version of the game.

Choose Your Arsenal Wisely

Based on where you are, what challenges you're currently encountering, and what you anticipate your needs will be, stock your backpack with the weapons and tools you believe you'll need. Don't forget you also need to stockpile appropriate weapons, ammo, loot items, and resources for the End Game.

At any time, your soldier's backpack can hold six items (including the pickaxe). That leaves five slots in which you can carry different types of guns, alternative weapons (such as Remote Explosives or Grenades), and/or loot (such as Med Kits, Chug Jugs, Shield Potions, Bandages, or Slurp Juice). Make smart inventory decisions throughout each match. The Backpack Inventory screen allows you to view what you have, plus organize the backpack's contents.

Some weapons, like pistols, are ideal for close-range firefights. Other weapons (like shotguns) are better suited for mid-range combat. Rifles with a scope and the more powerful, projectile explosive weapons (like rocket launchers or grenade launchers) are ideal for destroying structures and/or enemies from a distance. It's important to find and carry an assortment of weapons, so you're able to deal with any fighting situation you encounter.

Based on the location you're in, you can anticipate many of your weapon needs. For example, if you'll be fighting within homes, buildings, or structures, weapons best suited for close-range combat (and related ammo) will be needed.

As you prepare for the End Game, if your strategy is to build a fortress and shoot at enemies (and their fortresses) from the safety of your fortress, a selection of long-range weapons (a rifle with a scope and/or projectile explosive weapons) will be needed. Check out this sniper rifle with a scope that's on the ground waiting to be snatched up.

During a match, check your Backpack Inventory screen to learn more about each of the weapons you're carrying, and to determine how much of each type of ammunition you have on hand. To do this, access the Backpack Inventory screen and then highlight and select a weapon. Here, a pistol is selected and information about it is shown. From this screen, it's also possible to re-organize the backpack's contents, so it becomes faster and easier to grab the weapons or items you tend to use the most frequently.

heading on the right side of the screen, the Ammo: Heavy Bullets icon is selected. From the left side of the screen, you'll learn that these are high-caliber bullets used in sniper rifles. This soldier currently has six of these bullets on hand.

Here, the Ammo: Medium Bullets icon is highlighted and selected. You can see that this soldier has 26 of these bullets on hand, and that this type of ammo is used in mid-range weapons, such as assault rifles.

The various types of ammunition you've collected, how much of each ammo type you have on hand, and which weapons the ammo types can be used for, can also be displayed on the Backpack Inventory screen. While viewing this screen, select a specific ammunition type to learn more about it. Here, below the Ammo

By highlighting and selecting the Ammo Shells icon found on the right side of the Backpack Inventory screen, you'll see that this type of ammo is for guns that use shells, including shotguns. This soldier has eight rounds of shells on hand.

Rockets are a type of ammo used in conjunction with projectile explosive weapons. This type of weapon/ammo combination is ideal for destroying structures and shooting at enemies from a distance when you don't need the accuracy of using a scoped weapon.

During every match they experience, many expert players always place their favorite weapons within the same slots of their backpack, so they know exactly where they are, and can switch to them quickly when it's needed.

Learn How to Use a Sniper Rifle

To knock off an enemy with one shot using a sniper rifle takes some practice. How you aim this type of weapon will vary, based on the distance you are from the target. To inflict the most damage, always aim for a headshot.

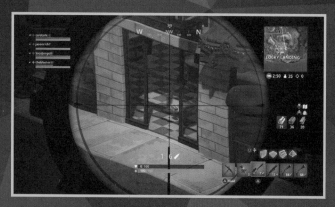

If the enemy is very far away, you don't necessarily want to center the target in your gun's crosshairs. When a target is far away, you'll need to aim slightly higher than your target in order to hit it. Use the ticks displayed in the scope's crosshairs to help you with this.

When using any type of sniper rifle with a scope, you also need to anticipate your target's movement, because once you pull the trigger, the bullet takes time to travel, and your target could move. If you're carrying two sniper rifles, position them side by side in your backpack. Then, instead of waiting for one to reload after you fire it, switch to the other gun, and you'll be able to shoot again faster.

There are YouTube videos produced by top-ranked *Fortnite: Battle Royale* players that specifically explain how to accurately aim different types of sniper rifles, based on the type of weapon and your distance from the enemy. To find these videos, type "Aiming Sniper Rifle Fortnite" into YouTube's Search field.

How and Where to Collect Ammo

There are several ways to find and collect ammo:

- It can sometimes be found out in the open, lying on the ground.
- It can be collected from enemies you defeat.
- It's offered within chests, Supply Drops, and Loot Llamas.
- It's offered within Ammo Boxes.

In addition to looking at the Backpack Inventory screen to check your current supply of ammo, when you look at the items you're carrying (shown here in the lower-right corner of the screen), the number in the bottom-right corner associated with each gun icon refers to how many rounds of ammo you're holding for that weapon. The location of where this information is displayed on the screen will vary, based on which gaming platform you're using.

Ammo Boxes are green. Unlike chests, they do not glow or make any sound. When you approach an Ammo Box and open it, a random assortment of ammo will pop out for you to collect. Sometimes, Ammo Boxes are found lying on the ground, out in the open (shown here).

You'll also often find Ammo Boxes or loose ammo hidden under staircases (shown here), behind objects, or on shelves, for example. Always grab ammo when you find it, even if you don't yet have a weapon that the ammo will work with. You're always better off stocking up on ammo, as opposed to running out of it during a firefight.

Be on the Constant Lookout for Chests, Supply Drops, and Loot Llamas

One of your first priorities once you and your teammates land on the island is to find weapons.

You'll often find small piles of ammo lying on the ground, out in the open (sometimes alongside weapons that you can grab). Here, you can see a pistol and related ammo by the picnic table.

Some weapons and ammo can be found lying out in the open (on the ground).

Throughout the island—mainly within buildings, homes, and other structures, as well as inside of trucks, but sometimes out in the open—you'll discover chests.

Chests have a golden glow and make a sound when you get close to them. Open chests to collect a random selection of weapons, ammo, loot items, and resources. To collect a chest's contents, you must be the first soldier to open it during a match.

Some chests are usually found at the same spot on the map match after match, although this is changing as Epic Games releases new game updates. Sometimes, chests randomly appear during each match, so always be on the lookout for them (and listen carefully for the sound they make).

Sometimes chests can be found in the back of trucks, like this one.

At random times during a match, you may be lucky enough to spot a Supply Drop. This is a floating balloon with a wooden crate attached. They're somewhat rare. If you spot one, approach with caution, and open the crate. Inside you'll discover a random selection of weapons, loot items, ammo, and resource icons.

As you're exploring various areas, listen closely for the unique sound chests emit. You'll often hear this sound before a chest comes into view. Assuming it's safe, approach the chest and open it. Then be ready to grab the items you want or need. Anytime you're searching a home, you'll often find one or more chests in an attic, basement, or garage.

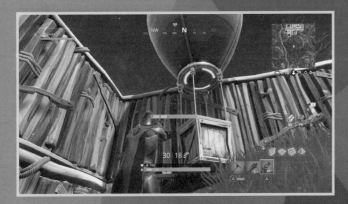

To protect yourself as you approach a Supply Drop (as well as a chest or Loot Llama) quickly build walls around yourself and the object.

Here, the Supply Drop was surrounded by three brick walls, and the soldier approaching it used a Bush to camouflage himself during his approach.

An even rarer object to come across on the island is a Loot Llama. This colorful item looks like a piñata. Smash it open and you'll discover a collection of random weapons, ammo, loot items, and resource icons. Typically, the weapons found within Loot Llamas are rare and often "legendary."

It's faster to smash open a Loot Llama with your pickaxe (by smacking it a few times) than it is to press the Search button on your controller or keyboard. Check out this random assortment of weapons, ammo, loot items, and resources that the Loot Llama provided. During each match, only three Loot Llamas appear on the island in random places.

Another strategy instead of opening a Loot Llama, for example, is to place remote explosives on it and then hide. As soon as an enemy soldier approaches, manually detonate the explosives to defeat the enemy. As you approach a Supply Drop or Loot Llama, consider quickly building walls around yourself and the object, so you're protected before opening the crate or smashing the Loot Llama.

Another way to quickly build up your arsenal is to buy rare and powerful weapons from Vending Machines. These can be found in random locations on the island. If you've gathered enough resources (wood, stone, or metal), exchange them for useful weapons or loot items.

If you don't yet have enough resources to purchase the item(s) you want, go out and collect more wood, stone, or metal, and then return to the Vending Machine. Keep in mind, when you're standing in front of a Vending Machine, you're vulnerable to attack.

Consider building walls to surround your soldier and the machine. Otherwise, as soon as you make a purchase, a nearby enemy might launch a surprise attack, defeat you, and quickly collect everything you've purchased and gathered during the match.

CHAPTER 5
GATHERING, USING, AND SHARING LOOT ITEMS

In addition to the wide range of weapons available to you, scattered throughout the island will be a random collection of loot items. Each loot item can serve one of three purposes:

- Recharge your soldier's Health and/or Shield meter.
- Serve as an explosive weapon that can be used against enemy soldiers, or to destroy structures.
- Help you travel around the island.

The available selection of loot items is continuously changing. Each time Epic Games releases a game update (patch), sometimes new loot items are introduced into the game, while others are "vaulted." A vaulted item is removed from the game but may be re-introduced at a later time. Periodically, the capability of a loot item is altered, making it more or less powerful.

As you and your teammates explore the island, you'll quickly discover that some loot items, like Bandages, are very common. They're found frequently and easy to use. Others are much rarer, so when you find a rare item, it's important to choose the very best time during a match to use them.

Some loot items require one of the slots in your soldier's backpack to store them for later use. Since you only have six slots capable of holding your pickaxe, choose carefully which loot items to use immediately, which to carry with you so they can be used later, and which need to be left behind for someone else (either your squad mate or an enemy) to use. Here, it's about midway through a match and the soldier has two Shield Potions, three Impulse Grenades, three types of guns (with a good amount of ammunition), and his trusty pickaxe.

- They're often found within chests, Supply Drops, and Loot Llamas.
- They can be taken from an enemy soldier who has been defeated and eliminated from the match.
- Some loot items can be purchased from Vending Machines.
- They can be traded between teammates.

Apples (which replenish 5 points of Health) and mushrooms (which replenish 5 points of Shields) can't be carried and stored for later use.

Discover the Selection of Loot Items Available on the Island

Here's information about many of the loot items potentially available to you on the island during a match. Keep in mind, when you play *Fortnite: Battle Royale*, you may come across newly introduced loot items not mentioned here or discover that some of the items listed here have been vaulted.

A few loot items, like Bushes, Traps, and Cozy Campfires, get stored with your resources, and become accessible from the Building menu, once you acquire them. These do not require a slot in your soldier's backpack. Shown here is a soldier using a Bush item. As you can see, he's almost entirely hidden within the bush.

Ways to Find and Gather Loot Items

Loot items can be acquired in the following ways:

- They can sometimes be found lying out in the open, on the ground.

All Terrain Karts (ATKs)—These golf cart vehicles represent a new and exciting way to travel around the island quickly. They can be found in several areas of the island, most notably Lazy Links, but they can be driven virtually anywhere—including off-road. Oh, and if you run over enemies, it causes them damage. If the hit and run doesn't cause serious injury, the enemy will likely shoot at you, so take evasive action and drive in a zigzag and unpredictable path.

Once you hop into an ATK and start driving, you're unable to fire a weapon until you switch back into Combat mode. This will require you to stand in the back of the vehicle or jump out of it. Memorize the controller or keyboard/mouse buttons used to drive an ATK. You'll need to practice climbing into the vehicle, switching seats, driving forward, driving in reverse, and performing power slides, for example.

Located near map coordinates J6.5 is a race-track. If you're driving an ATK, take it for a spin along the track to practice your driving skills. Just watch out for enemy shooters waiting to blow you off the track.

Apples—Found randomly under trees, pick up one apple at a time and consume it. Your Health meter will increase by 5 points (up to a maximum of 100). It is not possible to pick up and carry apples. They must be consumed when and where they're found.

The roof of an ATK can serve as a bounce pad, so you can leap high up into the air by stepping on it. Multiple squad members can ride in an ATK at once. If the vehicle goes airborne after going over a jump, lean back to go higher into the air.

Bandages—Each time a Bandage is used, it replenishes 15 HP (up to 100). A player can carry up to five bandages within their back-pack in a single slot.

It takes several seconds to use Bandages, during which time a soldier is vulnerable to attack, so be sure you're well-hidden or protected when using this item.

Use a Bouncer to quickly get high up and see what's around you, or to catapult your soldier upward and forward, to cover more territory faster. When strategically placed, a Bouncer can also be used like a Trap to slow down enemies.

Boogie Bombs—Toss one of these bombs at an opponent and they'll be forced to dance for five seconds while taking damage.

A Bouncer must be placed on a flat surface. If you need to, build a wooden floor tile first, and then place the Bouncer on top of it.

Bouncer—Place this pad on the ground, and whoever steps on it will get tossed into the air and receive zero damage from the resulting fall.

Bushes—A bush can be worn by a soldier and used as camouflage. Be sure to crouch to avoid being seen. If there are other bushes in the area, you'll blend right in. However, a bush offers no protection from attacks. If you start moving while camouflaged by a bush, an adversary will definitely notice and will likely attack.

Chug Jugs—This item takes 15 seconds to drink, during which time a soldier is vulnerable to attack unless he/she's protected. Consuming a Chug Jug restores a soldier's Health *and* Shield meter to 100 percent. Drink one of these as you enter later stages of a match, when survival becomes more difficult.

Clingers—When you throw one of these plunger-shaped grenades at an enemy, it sticks to them and explodes. Hold down the Aim button before tossing a Clinger (or a Grenade), and you'll see where it will land. This allows you to adjust your throwing angle as needed, to ensure the explosive you're throwing hits its intended target. Doing this takes a second or two longer but improves your accuracy. Throw multiple Clingers at the same target to inflict more damage.

This item is best used outside when standing still to avoid being detected by nearby enemies. There is a soldier using the Bush item and walking around here, directly in front of the soldier wearing the red Vertex outfit. As soon as a bush takes any damage, it disappears. It can also be dropped from the Backpack Inventory screen to make it go away.

Cozy Campfires—Once activated, any soldier that stands next to the fire will gain two HP per second, for up to 25 seconds (up to 50 HP).

The drawback is that a soldier is vulnerable to attack during this time, so activate the campfire after building a protective barrier around yourself and the campfire or find a secure and secluded place to use it. If you're playing with teammates, multiple people can take advantage of the campfire's healing powers. When you pile two Cozy Campfires on top of each other, you'll double its healing capabilities.

Grenades—Toss a grenade at an enemy, and it'll explode on impact. Direct hits cause the most damage, but even if the grenade lands close to an enemy, damage is still inflicted.

On the left is a structure before it was pummeled by three grenades.

Shown on the right is what remained of the structure after the grenades detonated.

Hop Rocks—Introduced during Season 4 and found inside craters caused by comets falling from space, when a soldier picks up and consumes a Hop Rock, he or she can temporarily jump higher, leap farther, and cover a lot more territory faster. After consuming a Hop Rock, your soldier will glow during the 30 seconds or so it's active. At the start of Season 5, Hop Rocks were vaulted. However, you never know when they could make a surprise return to the game.

Impulse Grenades—This type of grenade inflicts damage to enemies and throws them into the air, away from the point of impact.

Launch Pads—Activate this item to catapult your soldier into the air, and automatically utilize their glider. You can then guide them around in mid-air for a few seconds. Use this tool, for example, to escape after being engulfed by the storm, or to flee from an attack. It allows you to move great distances quickly. While you're flying, you can still be shot at by enemies. A Launch Pad must be built on a flat surface.

Mushrooms—Found randomly in swampy areas of the island, when your soldier picks up one blue mushroom at a time and consumes it, his or her Shield meter will increase by 5 points (up to a maximum of 100). It is not possible to pick up and carry mushrooms. They must be consumed when and where they're found.

Med Kits—Restore your health to 100 percent each time a Med Kit is used. It takes 10 seconds to use a Med Kit, during which time your solider is vulnerable to attack.

Port-A-Forts—This is a fort made of metal that instantly gets built when you activate it. Use it for protection without manually having to do any building. It requires no resources. Included within the Port-A-Fort are tires, allowing you to jump to the top of the fort (from the inside) with ease.

In addition to offering protection, the top of a fort provides an ideal vantage point for shooting enemies in any direction. Don't forget, any time you find tires on the island, jump onto them and you'll bounce up higher than you can jump yourself.

A Port-A-Fort has a weakness you might be able to exploit. If you're standing in front of an enemy who builds one, smash your pickaxe at the wall of the Port-A-Fort while it's being built, and you can break into it and then attack the enemy who built it from the inside.

When you're the one building a Port-A-Fort, leap to the top of it by bouncing on the tires, and then immediately build a metal floor below you. This will slow down any enemies who break in and try to attack from below.

Remote Explosives—A soldier can carry up to 10 of these explosives at once. Activate it by attaching it to an object, wall, or structure, for example, and detonate it remotely from any distance away. Detonate several at a time to create bigger explosions.

After setting up a remote explosive, lure your adversary to its location before detonating it. Just make sure you're far enough away to avoid the explosion yourself. Once activated, a Remote Explosive emits a flashing blue light until its detonated.

Shield Potions—Each time you drink a Shield Potion, your Shield meter increases by 50 (up to a maximum of 100). Drink two in a row to fully activate and replenish your soldier's shields. This item takes several seconds to consume, during which time your soldier is vulnerable to attack.

Shopping Carts—These items come and go from the game. If you come across one on the island, you can push it up a hill (or a ramp you build) and then ride it down.

Riding a Shopping Cart is a faster way to travel around the island. It allows you to cover more territory and is faster than walking or running.

Slurp Juice—As you drink this item, your Health and Shield meters increase by one point every second (for up to 25 seconds). While you're drinking, your soldier must be standing still and is vulnerable to attack.

Small Shield Potions—Consuming this item increases your shield strength by 25, but it

takes several seconds to drink, during which time your soldier is vulnerable to attack.

Stink Bomb—Toss one of these grenades at your enemies, and they will quickly be surrounded by a cloud of yellow stink. For every half-second they remain engulfed in the cloud, their Health meter is reduced by 5 points. The yellow stink cloud lasts for a total of nine seconds before it disappears, but an enemy can potentially escape from the cloud sooner. For maximum results, throw multiple Stink Bombs at the same target to create a bigger cloud.

Traps—Set a Trap on any structure's floor, wall, or ceiling and then leave it. They can also be placed on ramps. When an opponent accidently activates a Trap, he or she will receive mega-damage. Just make sure you don't set off the Trap yourself once you've activated it, or you'll be the one getting hurt!

Position Traps where they can't easily be seen by your enemies, so they walk right into them and set them off. Use Traps to boobytrap rooms, small areas, ramps, or fortresses. Several different types of Traps can be found and used.

In some cases, multiples of the same item can be stored together within a single slot of a soldier's backpack. For example, you can carry several Shield Potions simultaneously, and then use them one at a time, as they're needed. Here, look in the lower-right corner of the screen where your backpack inventory is displayed and you'll see this soldier collected and is carrying 10 Bandages.

CHAPTER 6
EXPERT BUILDING STRATEGIES

No matter which *Fortnite: Battle Royale* game play mode you're experiencing, in order to reach otherwise inaccessible areas, and to protect yourself from incoming attacks, you'll often need to build ramps/stairs, bridges, structures, and fortresses using the resources (wood, stone, and metal) you've collected. Once you understand how Building mode works, you need to keep practicing your building skills, so that you master the art of quick and efficient building.

Becoming an expert builder in *Fortnite: Battle Royale* is one of the most difficult skills to master. In addition to Solo, Duos, and Squads, if the Playground game play mode is available, this offers the perfect place to practice your building skills, without the threat of being attacked. Playground mode is periodically offered by Epic Games on a temporary basis.

During an actual match, once you decide when building is necessary, you'll need to quickly decide what to build, which material to build with, and where to build. Each teammate can assist with the building if they're nearby. Teammates can also share resources to help the person assigned to building construct the strongest structures or fortresses possible.

Ways to Gather the Resources You'll Need

The more resources you harvest or collect during a match, the more building you'll be able to do. Without resources, however, you're unable to build anything. At the start of a match, you'll have zero resources. You're ultimately able to hold a maximum of 1,000 wood, 1,000 stone, and 1,000 metal at any given time.

When playing most versions of *Fortnite: Battle Royale*, the amount of wood, stone, and metal you current have is displayed along the right side of the screen. Look for the wood, stone, and metal icons with numbers below them. (The location may vary based on the gaming platform you're using.)

During a match, there are five primary ways to harvest and collect wood, stone, and metal including:

1. Use your soldier's pickaxe to smash objects and harvest resources.
2. Collect resource icons. They can be found out in the open (often lying on the ground).
3. Defeat an enemy and collect the resources he or she was carrying. Especially during the later stages of a match, this is a quick way to really increase your resources.
4. Collect resource icons from chests, Supply Drops, and Loot Llamas. Each of these will significantly boost your resources.
5. Receive resources from one or more teammates.

As you're smashing bigger trees, only harvest between 50 and 75 percent of their wood and leave the tree standing. When a large tree falls from being harvested, it can be seen from all around, and this could reveal your location to nearby enemies. By abandoning the tree before it's fully harvested, you'll receive slightly less wood, but the tree remains standing and you can move to the next one. Keep an eye on the HP meter for the tree as you're smashing it with your pickaxe, so you know when to stop.

Anything made of wood that you smash will generate wood resources. Trees, wooden pallets, and the walls or floors of many houses, buildings, and structures are all great sources of wood. The larger the tree and the thicker its truck, the more wood you'll harvest by smashing it. Wood is the most abundant and easily accessible resource on the island.

To quickly boost your collection of wood (and other resources), start smashing anything within a house or building, including the furniture.

Smashing rock formations with the pickaxe is one way to generate stone (bricks). You can also smash brick buildings or other stone objects.

Smashing metal objects, including appliances in homes, machinery in buildings, any type of vehicle, or large metal storage containers, are all great sources of metal.

This is what a Wood icon looks like. Grab it and, in this case, your wood resource goes up

by 20. This is indicated by the yellow tag in the top-right corner of the banner that describes the Wood icon the soldier is about to grab.

When you come across a Stone icon (which looks like a brick), grab it. You'll receive a small bundle of that resource. The small yellow icon displayed on the item name banner says how much of the resource you'll collect. In this case, it's x20 stone, which is typical for resource icons found lying out in the open, on the ground, for example.

Find and grab Metal icons to increase your stash of metal.

Resources can easily be shared with team-mates. To do this, access your Backpack Inventory screen. Select and highlight the resource you want to share (wood, stone, or metal). Press the Drop button on the control-ler/keyboard. This pop-up window will appear. Use the slider to determine how much of the selected resource you want to share. Here, 53 wood (out of 256 that the soldier is holding) will be shared. Press the Drop button to drop the selected amount of that resource for your nearby teammate to pick up.

Building Strategies You Need to Master

In order to build, you'll need to put away your weapons (and pickaxe) and enter into Building mode. Switching between Combat and Building mode is done by pressing the appropriate game controller button (or the appropriate keyboard or mouse button if you're playing on a computer).

Once in Building mode, there are two choices you'll need to make immediately. First, which resource you want to build with. Second, which shape building tile you want to create. By mixing and matching the four building tile shapes, you can build walls, ramps/stairs, bridges, basic fortress, or extremely elaborate

structures, depending on your need, creativ-ity, and available resources.

Hold down the Build key on the controller (or keyboard/mouse) to activate the game's Turbo Building feature and be able to build even faster. Like everything else related to building, using the Turbo Building feature effectively requires practice.

When an enemy soldier is building (or they're in building mode and preparing to build), they can't use a weapon, so they're vulnera-ble to attack for those few seconds it takes to switch from Building mode back to Combat mode. Take advantage of this if you're the one attacking.

Many of the screenshots in this chapter were taken within the Playground game play mode.

The four building tile shapes include:

Vertical wall tiles. After selecting a building resource and a tile shape, a translucent ver-sion of the building tile is displayed. Use the directional controls to choose the desired location to place the tile, before pressing the Build button.

As soon as you press the Build button, the selected and positioned tile is built using the chosen material. At this point, while still in Building mode, have your soldier face the tile and enter into Edit mode to alter that tile. For example, you can add a door or window to a wall tile or make a hole within a ceiling or floor tile.

While the building tile is still translucent, the information displayed near the center of the tile before it's actually built tells you how much of the selected resource is needed to build that tile. A vertical wood wall requires 10 wood to build. You'll also discover that once built, the vertical wall tile will have 200 HP. While the selected building tile is still translucent, you can still reposition it, rotate it, or change the building material using your controller or keyboard commands.

This is a wooden ramp tile being positioned before it's actually built. When building with wood, and the ramp/stairs-shaped tile is selected, ramps are automatically constructed.

Shown here is a single ramp tile. It goes up one level. Use this type of tile to quickly reach a higher up area that's otherwise difficult to reach, or to gain a height advantage over your opponent.

Here, a single floor/ceiling tile is actually in the process of being built out of wood.

As you're walking (or running) up the ramp, keep building to get higher. During the few seconds it takes to build a wooden tile, it's less vulnerable to an attack than a metal tile. If you shoot a metal tile while it's being built, you can often destroy it. (Obviously, it's harder to destroy a metal tile once it's fully constructed.)

Here, a single ramp tile was used within a house in order to go from the top floor to the attic. After climbing the ramp, this soldier will use his pickaxe to smash through the ceiling and discover the chest. From where this soldier is standing below the chest, the unique sound effect the chest generates can be heard, even though the chest can't be seen.

By building this ramp out of metal and placing it over the stairs in the house, it'll slow down any enemies trying to get upstairs. When a metal ramp (staircase) is fully built, it will have 370 HP. It costs 10 metal per tile to build.

As soon as you start building any tile, the tile's HP meter is displayed, and that tile begins offering protective shielding against an attack. The HP meter starts out displayed in orange to show the tile is not completed. It then turns green when it's been fully constructed. Remember, until the tile is fully constructed, it does not have its full HP, so it does not offer its maximum protection. Here, the partially built metal staircase currently offers 242 HP out of 280 HP.

When building with stone or metal, after selecting the ramp/stairs tile shape, stairs are automatically constructed, but at a slower rate. Anything built with stone is stronger than wood, and anything built with metal is even stronger. This stone staircase, for example, offers 280 HP. Each stone tile in this staircase required 10 stone to construct.

Pyramid-shaped tiles that can be used to hide behind, or as a roof for your structures and fortresses. This type of tile made from wood offers 190 HP and costs 10 wood each to construct. If the same tile shape were built from stone, once completed, it could withstand 280 HP worth of damage. One pyramid-shaped tile made with metal (which costs 10 metal to build), however, can withstand 370 HP worth of damage. Thus, pyramid tiles made of metal provide excellent shielding from an incoming attack.

This wooden structure was built using one floor tile, and four vertical wall tiles. One pyramid-shaped tile was used for the roof. Once the core structure was built, a door was then added, making it easy for the soldier to enter and exit.

This is the same basic structure, but it's made out of metal. When facing one of the walls, you can see it'll withstand 400 HP worth of damage, which is twice the strength of the wood version.

Ramp-Building Techniques

One of the most basic structures you're able to build, and the one you're likely to use most

frequently, is a multi-tile ramp that goes up two or more levels. This ramp was constructed using multiple wood ramp/stair tiles. The more tiles you use, the taller your ramp (or staircase) becomes, but the more resources you'll need to build it.

The main drawback to building and using a tall ramp is that an enemy can shoot at and destroy the bottom tile (or any tile in the middle), and the whole ramp will fall apart and crash to the ground, with you standing on it. If you fall more than three levels, you'll perish.

Building a ramp next to a cliff makes the ramp stronger, so it can't be shot at and destroyed as easily.

As you're building a ramp and walking or running up it at the same time, position the Building icon in front of you (instead of downward) to build a ramp with a second ramp above you.

This overhead ramp builds at the same time and offers protection from above. This strategy uses twice the resources, but in some situations, the additional shielding is well worth it.

If you think an enemy is going to run up your ramp and follow you, as you're building the ramp, take an extra few seconds to add one horizontal floor tile, and then place a Trap on top of it. Continue building the ramp upward. When the enemy steps on the Trap . . . BOOM!

How to Build Basic Fortresses

Another common strategy is to build a double ramp. This allows your soldier to zip-zag between ramps as he or she is climbing. If one ramp is about to collapse after being attacked, the soldier on the ramp can leap to the other, and potentially avoid a fatal fall.

Build a bridge the same way you'd build a ramp but use the horizontal wall tile instead of a ramp/stair-shaped tile.

Another basic structure you'll definitely want to become a pro at building very quickly is four walls around yourself. This is done using four vertical wall tiles and the directional controls on your controller or keyboard.

Surround yourself with walls when someone is shooting at you, you need to heal yourself, revive another soldier, open a chest, open a Loot Llama, open a Supply Drop, or use a Vending Machine.

When you come across a chest, Loot Llama (shown here), or Supply Drop that's out in the open, or when an enemy is shooting at you, quickly surrounding yourself with walls will offer shielding, at least for a few extra seconds, so you can escape or regroup. However, with the right weapons, an enemy can typically destroy your structures, especially if they're made from wood. Here, metal walls were built around the chest.

A wooden wall can withstand just 200 HP worth of damage before being destroyed. A stone wall can withstand 300 HP worth of damage from an incoming attack, while a metal wall (shown here surrounding the chest) can withstand 400 HP of damage from an incoming attack.

When you collect Traps, Cozy Campfires, Launch Pads, and certain other loot items, they do not take up slots within your backpack's inventory. Instead, these items become accessible from Building mode. To use these items, they must be stored in your backpack's inventory, and then selected from the Building menu.

Here, near the bottom-right corner of the screen, notice the Trap icon that's displayed to the right of the four building tile options is selected. A Trap has been selected from the Building menu and is now being placed within a house.

A Launch Pad, which also gets stored with a soldier's resources, not in a backpack inventory slot, is shown on the previous page. It's been selected from the Building menu and is about to be placed on a floor tile that's already been constructed.

When you're out in the open and being shot at, one quick structure you can build is a vertical wall, with a ramp placed directly behind it. Now you can crouch down behind this structure and have two layers of protection that an enemy must destroy in order to reach you. Again, building with wood is the fastest. If you build with metal, for example, the structure will ultimately offer more protection but until it's fully built, it'll offer less protection and you could still be vulnerable to an attack during the building process.

If you want to climb up the ramp to peek out over the top and shoot back at your enemies, consider building walls on the side to protect you against flank attacks.

How to Build a 1x1 Fortress

A 1x1 fortress is simply four walls around you, with a ramp in the center, that goes up multiple levels. Using wood allows you to build with the greatest speed, but using metal offers the greatest protection. Keep practicing until you're able to build this type of fortress very quickly, without having to think too much about it.

Here's how to build a 1x1 fortress:

Especially if you're building on an uneven surface, consider starting with a floor tile on the ground.

Next, build four vertical walls so they surround you. Using metal is ideal.

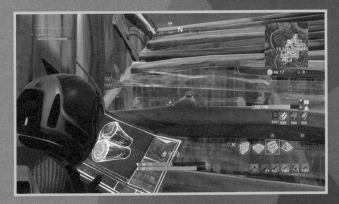

In the center, build a ramp. As the ramp is being constructed, jump on it.

Keep repeating this process to add levels to your fort. You can build as high as you need to, but in most situations, three or four levels is adequate.

At the top, consider adding pyramid-shaped roof pieces all around the roof for added protection when you peek out. However, if you need protection from directly above as well,

add a flat roof or a pyramid-shaped roof piece directly over your head.

Surrounding the top of the 1x1 fort with pyramid-shaped tiles gives you objects to hide behind if you're peeking out from the top in order to shoot at enemies below.

This is what a three-level 1x1 fortress looks like from the outside. Keep in mind, because it's made of wood (and not stone or metal), it would offer limited protection from an incoming attack, especially if more powerful explosive weapons are used to attack and attempt to destroy it.

How to Use Edit Mode to Add Windows, Doors, and More

Once you've built a structure out of wood, metal, and/or stone, you're able to enter into Edit mode to modify certain tiles, such as walls, floors, or ceilings. This is useful if you want to add a door or window or create an opening.

To enter into Edit mode, face a building tile that's been constructed. Shown here is one of the bottom walls of a 1x1 fortress. Press the appropriate controller or keyboard/mouse button to enter into Edit mode. The controller or keyboard key you need to press will be displayed above the Edit icon that appears.

Once in Edit mode, the building tile you're facing turns blue and is divided into segments.

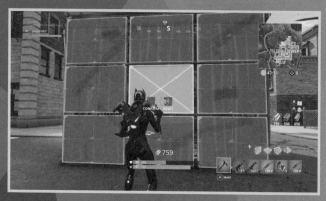

Using the directional controls, start by pointing to one segment (box) and use the trigger to select it. If you're building a window, you're all set. Simply use the Confirm command to create the window. However, to build a door, you'll need to highlight and select two squares of the building tile (one on top of the other). To continue building a door, select the second square on the tile, either above or below the first one you selected. With both tiles selected, press the Confirm option.

In a few seconds, the door will be built. You're now able to open and close it, just as you would any other door in the game. Keep in mind, anyone else who approaches can also open the door to enter your structure.

Learning how to build, and then practicing until you're able to build extremely quickly is essential. Equally important, however, is to practice using Edit mode, so you're able to modify your structures quickly and efficiently during matches.

This is what a window looks like when it's built into a vertical wall. Use a window to peek out, or to point your weapon and snipe at enemies. Anytime you build a window into a structure, just as you can see and shoot out, your enemies can see in and shoot through the window to attack you.

While in Building mode, you can clear four out of nine squares, for example, in order to create an arched opening.

This type of arched opening provides an easy way to expand your structure outwards with additional building. Of course, until you've done the additional building, the large opening within the structure leaves you potentially vulnerable to an incoming attack, with no protection except for your soldier's own health and shields.

After creating a multi-level structure or fortress, use Edit mode to create a hole in the floor or ceiling (when a flat floor/ceiling file was used), so you can quickly drop downward or climb upward. When in Edit mode, build a one-box window in the floor or ceiling tile.

Keep in mind, explosive weapons can destroy structures, often much faster than enemy bullets. So, if an enemy tosses a grenade or launches a rocket from a rocket launcher, the structure you're in could crumble around you. As a result of the explosion, you could be injured or even perish from the explosion.

Use Your Creativity to Build More Elaborate Structures

Taking full advantage of the four different-shaped building tiles and Edit mode, use your own creativity to come up with structure designs that:

- Provide protection from incoming attacks.
- Offer a good view of your surroundings from the top.
- Allow you to be higher up than your opponents, so you can shoot at them from above.
- Provide a place to safely hide, so you can use loot items to replenish your health and shields prior to launching an attack. If you need to revive a teammate, build walls around you both before using revive, so you're not vulnerable to attack.
- Use a weapon with a scope to accurately shoot at enemies from a distance, while being protected.

In addition to doing your own experimentation, one excellent strategy for obtaining the best structure design ideas is to watch other players.

Another option is to watch YouTube videos produced by expert *Fortnite: Battle Royale* players, or to watch live streams of highly ranked players participating in matches on Twitch.tv. When you do this, pay extra attention to their building technique as they enter into the End Game portion of a match.

Building Advice When Preparing for the End Game

It's a common End Game strategy for players who make it into the Final Circle to build a large and sturdy fortress from which they can launch attacks on the remaining enemy soldiers using projectile explosive weapons, such as a grenade launcher or rocket launcher.

In order to build an elaborate fortress, and be able to repair it as needed during the match, you'll need to collect an abundance of resources. Plan ahead! If possible, collect or harvest 1,000 wood, 1,000 stone, and up to 1,000 metal prior to entering into the End Game. The longer you wait to collect the needed resources, the more dangerous it becomes, because you'll be in closer proximity to skilled enemies who will attack you while you're harvesting resources.

Along with having adequate levels of resources, make sure that within your backpack's inventory you have the loot items and weapons you'll need to launch attacks (such as a weapon with a scope or a projectile explosive weapon). Be sure to replenish your health and shields as needed, so you can survive longer.

About halfway through each match, start thinking about the End Game and preparing for it. By defeating enemies in the later stages of a match, but prior to the End Game, you're able to grab all of the weapons, ammo, loot items, and resources that they've collected. This is a great way to build your arsenal and ensure you go into the End Game nicely equipped with resources.

If you haven't collected the powerful weapons you'll need during the End Game, and you don't necessarily want to risk engaging in battles before you absolutely have to, consider finding and using Vending Machines to stock up on weapons and needed loot items. Making purchases from Vending Machines requires using some of your resources, so plan accordingly.

How and Where to Build Your Final Fortress

If you make it into the End Game, your teammates may or may not still be around to assist you in your victory. Even if three of your squad mates have already perished earlier in a match, you can still use your own fighting and building skills to win a match and achieve #1 Victory Royale. However, if one or more of your teammates is still alive and active, this will increase your chance for victory, because

you can coordinate attacks with your surviving teammate(s).

As you enter into the Final Circle and the End Game portion of a match begins, you'll be in relatively close proximity to the most skilled and cunning gamers remaining in the match. The Final Circle will be relatively small, so it's essential that you choose the best possible location to build your fortress.

Do not build in the center of the Final Circle. While this will give you 360-degree access to enemies around you, it'll also make you the center of attention, and the first enemy that the remaining soldiers will simultaneously attack. You're much better off choosing a location that's not centralized, so you can hang back a bit while the remaining soldiers fight amongst themselves and use up their ammunition and remaining resources. Then you can launch your attacks on whoever is left.

If you have a weapon with a scope in your arsenal, use it to zoom in and spy on your enemies from a distance, and then plan your strategy for attack. Using a weapon with an infrared scope attached allows you to see an enemy's heat signature, even if you can't actually see the enemy hiding behind an object, for example.

You'll often need to build with your back to the storm. Don't forget, soldiers can remain alive in the storm for short periods of time, so it's possible for someone to enter into the storm on purpose in order to reposition themselves in a way that they can emerge from the storm and sneak up behind you to launch a surprise attack. (You can do the same to your opponents.)

As you're choosing a design for your final fortress, make sure you can see immediately below you. It's common for enemies to leave the safety of their own fortress and to rush enemy fortresses in order to launch close-range attacks with their most powerful weapons. Knowing this is a possibility, your arsenal should include at least one powerful weapon that's effective at close- to mid-range.

Consider placing a Launch Pad within your fortress. When you step on the Launch Pad, your soldier will fly upward. This allows you to get a bird's eye view of your surroundings and determine where the final few enemy soldiers may be hiding. While in the air, travel straight up, look around, and then drop back down into your fortress.

If you get yourself into a pinch during the End Game, and your fortress gets destroyed (but you manage to escape), or you forgot to collect enough resources to build a proper fortress, this is when using a Port-A-Fort can come in extremely handy.

End Game Strategies for Defending, Repairing, or Abandoning Your Fortress

Each tile your structures or fortresses are built with has a specific HP that translates directly to the level of damage it can withstand before getting demolished. Keeping this in mind, if the fortress you build during the End Game is not built with metal, it likely will not be able to withstand a direct hit from a projectile explosive weapon.

While inside a fortress or structure, if it gets attacked, you'll typically have a few seconds to decide if you want to rebuild and repair the damage as it occurs or evacuate the structure altogether.

If you stick around and try to quickly rebuild, while in Building mode, you can't use any weapons, so four factors need to be considered.

- Do you have enough resources to rebuild and repair the damage?
- Can you very quickly switch between Building mode and Combat mode, so you can counter-attack enemies, especially if someone is rushing your fortress?
- Do you have the right weapons (and ammo) on hand to defend yourself?
- Will you be able to maintain a height advantage if you keep building, repairing, and defending your fortress?

Depending on how savvy your final opponents are, you may find yourself in an extremely small Final Circle. In this situation, it may become a vertical battle, as one enemy will literally be on top of the other(s). Having the height advantage will help here but having a powerful short-range weapon that you're really good at aiming with will often allow you to win the match.

If your fortress gets destroyed, or you choose to forego building one during the End Game, you can still win the match. In this situation, you'll need to rush enemy fortresses, one at a time, and engage in close-range battles. Having grenades, clingers, and other explosives will help, as will powerful weapons that are good at close- to mid-range. The trick is to tiptoe as you approach an enemy fortress, so hopefully you won't be seen or heard.

In an effort to make fortress building less essential, especially during the End Game portion of a match, Epic Games has tweaked the HP strength of each shaped building tile, making wood a weaker material to build with, and stone or metal a stronger material to build with.

Wood continues to be useful for quickly building ramps and bridges, for example, but offers minimal protection when building fortresses or structures your soldier will use for defense against an incoming attack. While these HP ratings will likely change again, this is what they were near the end of Season 5:

TILE SHAPE	WOOD	STONE	METAL
Horizontal Floor/Ceiling Tile	140 HP	280 HP	460 HP
Vertical Wall Tile	150 HP	300 HP	500 HP
Ramp/Stairs Tile	140 HP	280 HP	460 HP
Pyramid-Shaped Tile	140 HP	280 HP	460 HP

CHAPTER 7
PROVEN STRATEGIES FOR WINNING MATCHES

Regardless of whether you're left alone on the island to fend for yourself after your teammates have been defeated (or you're playing Solo mode), or you have one or more teammates by your side as you confront enemy soldiers, here are some tips that'll help you stay alive longer.

Prepare Yourself for Whatever Terrain You Encounter

Whether you're exploring one of the labeled points of interest on the map, or you're traveling in between points of interest in order to avoid the storm or to explore, you're going to encounter many different types of terrain.

Anytime you need to travel across open terrain, where you're vulnerable to attack, run in a random, zig-zag pattern (don't walk), and keep jumping to make yourself a fast-moving target that's harder to hit. If you do start getting shot at, quickly hide behind a nearby object or build protective walls around yourself to serve as shielding.

Anytime you enter a building, house, or structure, be ready to explore. Inside, you'll likely find chests, as well as weapons, ammo, loot items, and/or resource icons lying out in the open. Within houses, chests are most often found in the attic, basement, or garage. Weapons, ammo, loot items, and resource icons are more typically found lying on the ground, out in the open, within various rooms.

Whenever you notice an outside cellar door as you approach a house, smash it open and explore the basement. You're almost guaranteed to find a chest, along with other weapons, ammo, loot items, and perhaps resource icons lying out in the open.

Inside homes, buildings, or structures, don't be surprised if you encounter enemy soldiers. As you enter a building, listen carefully for footsteps, as well as for the opening and closing of doors, or for items being smashed. If you hear someone else inside, you have several options. For example, you can:

- Leave the area and find someplace else to explore.
- Enter with your weapon drawn and be prepared to engage in battle.
- Peek through a window and shoot at an enemy from outside, or toss a grenade,

clinger, or another explosive weapon through the window.

- Wait outside, preferably hidden, and then attack the enemy as he or she leaves.

Instead of entering a building, house, or structure using the front door, consider entering through a back door or the garage, if applicable, so maybe you can surprise whoever is inside. Keep in mind, the inside of structures offers many potential hiding places.

After you enter into a structure or an individual room, close the door behind you. Then, if you anticipate an enemy soldier following you,

hide behind an object, crouch down, and aim your weapon toward the door. As soon as the enemy enters, start shooting.

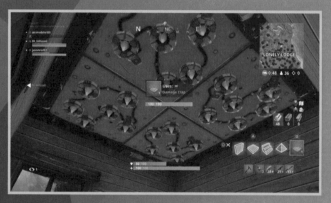

Another option is to booby trap a room within a house, building, or structure, using Remote Explosives or Traps, for example. Then, when an enemy enters, they'll receive a surprise blast. Just make sure you're far enough away from the explosion, so you don't get injured by your own explosive weapon attack.

Before entering a house or building, tiptoe up to a window and peek inside. If you see enemies lurking about, shoot at them through the window.

From outside of a house, building, or structure, throw grenades through a window, an open door, or hole in a wall or ceiling to blow up whoever is already inside (and to destroy the structure itself). Just make sure your soldier doesn't get caught in the blast as well. Here, the aiming crosshair is positioned in the center of the window, so grenades will be tossed inside, through the window.

It's also possible to build a ramp or fortress on top of a pre-existing structure.

Just about anything you encounter on the island can be smashed with the pickaxe, shot at (and destroyed if you hit it with enough ammo), or demolished using explosives. This includes buildings, homes (or parts of homes), and other structures.

Don't forget, you're able to build ramps, walls, or use other building tiles inside of pre-existing structures, or you can build onto an existing structure. For example, you can build a ramp to help you reach an attic that's otherwise not accessible from inside (shown here), or you can build a mini-fortress around yourself in the middle of a room.

By using the pickaxe to smash objects, such as the house's garage door, to get past an obstacle, you simultaneously harvest resources (wood, stone, or metal). However, if you blow something up with an explosive weapon or shoot at it in order to destroy it, you won't collect any resources. You will, however, clear away the obstacle.

Whenever you're about to open a door to or within a structure that may already be inhabited, have your weapon drawn and be ready to fire. Scan the room quickly, grab what you want if there's something worthwhile inside, and then move on to the next room.

When exploring a multi-story building, be sure to enter all of the rooms to discover what might be available to grab within them. Some buildings, houses, and churches, for example, have hidden rooms. You'll sometimes need to use the pickaxe to smash through walls, floors, or ceilings to discover these rooms, and then see what's inside.

Instead of traveling at ground level across wide open terrain, consider building a ramp to get yourself higher up, and then build a bridge that takes you in the direction you need to go. For example, build a ramp between the roofs of two or more buildings. This will require a bunch of resources, but it'll potentially keep you higher than your adversaries, which gives you a tactical advantage in a firefight.

When visiting certain areas, expect to encounter large piles of demolished cars, which create a maze-like area to navigate through at ground level. There are also storage facilities on the island that contain many large cargo containers. These too create maze-like areas. Try to avoid staying on ground level. Climb on top of the car piles or cargo containers, so you can shoot at enemies below you and see all around.

The ground level of maze-like areas is a great place to plan and execute sneak attacks or to ambush enemies. You can also set Traps or use remote explosives to blow up enemies who pass by.

Remember, anytime you approach a house, building, or structure, and you notice the front door is already open, someone else has been there before you, and they could be hiding inside and waiting to attack you. Plus, any chests, Ammo Boxes, or other loot items that were in the structure have likely already been rummaged through.

In many places on the island, you'll encounter cabins and other small, stand-alone structures. Hide inside any of them and close the door behind you. As soon as an enemy opens the door, be ready to blast them with one of your most powerful guns. Another strategy is to place a Trap inside one of these smaller structures, set it, and then close the door (if applicable) as you leave. The next person will be greeted with a bang!

If you opt to directly cross a large body of water, don't just walk through it. This will be very slow and leave you out in the open and vulnerable to attack. Instead, build a wooden bridge to cross it, and then move quickly. Be ready to build walls around yourself as shielding if you get shot at by someone sniping you from land. Instead of crossing the lake yourself, if you have a sniper rifle (or any weapon with a scope), find a secure hiding spot along the edge of the lake (or swamp), and then pick off other soldiers that attempt to cross when they're out in the open and fully exposed.

Don't get too distracted by exploration. Always pay attention to the location of the storm and the direction it'll be moving next. Here, the soldier is just outside the inner circle, where the storm will be expanding to next. Since you're able to survive in the storm for short periods of time, assuming your Health meter isn't close to being depleted, you can enter into the storm on purpose, and then reemerge outside of the storm, behind an opponent, to launch a surprise attack. Hide within the storm to reposition yourself, if necessary.

A good gamer will know to watch their back when it's to the storm, but a noob won't expect someone to exit from the storm with the sole purpose of attacking. If you need to travel a great distance quickly, to avoid an attack or outrun the storm, for example, consider using a Launch Pad or a Shopping Cart. When you step onto a Launch Pad, you get catapulted into the air, and can travel a far distance. Your glider will activate and allow you to steer your soldier safely back to land. A Rift-to-Go or Bouncer Pad can also be used to transport your soldier quickly or to help him jump from a high-up area and land on ground unhurt.

Just about anywhere on the island, to get a bird's eye view of what's around you, and to get higher up than enemies, consider building a ramp. Fortify the bottom of the ramp, so if an enemy tries to destroy it, you won't instantly come crashing down. Use a weapon with a scope to zoom in and see what your enemies are up to, and when they become visible, shoot 'em.

Anytime you're in an area that contains shops or restaurants, always check behind the counters. You never know what's waiting to be collected.

To reach a house's attic easily, land on its roof (shown here), build a ramp from the outside, or from the inside, start at ground level and work your way upward.

It is often easier to reach the outside of a house's roof and then smash your way into the attic from above.

Bridges that lead in and out of points of interest are often places where you're apt to stumble upon chests, as well as weapons, ammo, loot items, and/or resource icons that are lying out in the open. Search below the bridges as well.

Anytime you discover a water tower or a silo, smash it. You'll typically find a chest or other useful weapons. You'll also stock up on some metal by smashing the tower or silo.

There are several suburban communities found throughout the island that contain groups of single-family houses (along with other smaller structures). Search each home as you see fit and to build up your arsenal, but beware of enemy soldiers hiding out inside.

Instead of traveling along ground level to move between houses that are close together, go to a higher level (or the roof) and build a bridge between two houses or structures, so you can stay up high.

Wherever your exploration takes you on the island, when you encounter broken-down cars, trucks, RVs, tractors, buses, or other types of vehicles, you have the option to smash them and harvest metal.

Hiding behind any type of vehicle when you're being shot at or trying to avoid enemy contact is another way to take advantage of the many broken-down vehicles found on the island.

Remember, when you smash cars, it makes a lot of noise. To make matters worse, the car's alarm will often activate and generate even more noise. This will definitely attract attention and alert nearby enemies to your location.

Be sure to check within and above the larger trucks and vehicles for chests or other weapons, and then decide if you want to harvest some metal by smashing these larger vehicles.

There are places on the island that contain underground tunnels (or mine shafts). The tunnels have a maze-like design, so you can't see around turns. Listen carefully for footsteps. Don't get surprised and attacked by enemies. It's best to crouch down and tiptoe through these areas with your weapon drawn, so you make the least amount of noise possible, but you remain ready for a firefight.

In popular and heavily congested places, like Tilted Towers, it's dangerous to be outside and at ground level, because enemies can shoot at you from the higher levels of buildings that surround you. If you find yourself on ground level in a densely populated area, be ready to crouch behind vehicles or objects for protection if someone starts shooting at you.

Instead of staying at ground level, you're typically better off staying inside a building, as high up as possible. The roof of a building can also offer a great vantage point. Using your mid- to long-range weapons (preferably with a scope), look out a window and shoot at enemies below from a safe distance. Don't forget, you can shoot or be shot at through windows. Enemy soldiers can also enter the building you're in at any time, so if your back will be to a door inside, consider building a wall for extra shielding in case someone tries to enter.

As you explore the island, you'll encounter many steep cliffs. Never jump off a cliff. You could injure yourself or even perish. Instead, slide down the edge of a cliff, and you'll land safely on the ground.

Shopping Carts are rare, but if you find one, you can push it up a hill, hop into it, and then ride it down a hill and cover a lot of territory quickly. Shopping Carts have been added and removed from the game multiple times, and what can be done with them continues to change periodically.

When traveling through the dense forest areas of the island, smash down trees to collect wood. Also keep your eye out for apples on the ground. If you spot an apple, grab it and eat it. This will replenish 5 points (up to 100) on your soldier's Health meter. When in swampy areas, look for blue mushrooms on the ground. These will replenish 5 points (up to 100) on your soldier's Shield meter.

All Terrain Karts (ATKs) are souped-up golf carts that can be driven anywhere around the island. Each can hold up to four passengers and provides a fast way to get around. You'll find these vehicles randomly parked around the island. They are very common in and around Paradise Palms and Lazy Links.

Anytime you stumble across a pile of tires, you can't smash or collect them, but you can jump on them. When you jump on tires, you're catapulted up extra high into the air.

When you come across a rare weapon, like a rifle with a scope, or a rocket launcher, always grab it, even if you don't need it right away. These long-range weapons will definitely be useful later in the match. Once you have one of these powerful weapons, be sure to collect plenty of ammo for it.

Additional Strategies When Exploring with Teammates

The following are additional strategies that'll help teams and squads stay alive longer during matches.

Anytime you use the Fill feature after selecting the Duos or Squads game play mode, you'll often have at least one noob added to your team. If you find this annoying, select the Don't Fill option and hand pick your team members. Choose players with great game stats, and that complement your particular gaming style and skill set.

Once the team is established, choose a landing location that's *not* right in the heart of a popular point of interest. This will give you extra time to build up your collective arsenal before having to engage in battle. All too often, squads land in a point of interest they know will be populated by hordes of enemies. As a result, several squad members often wind up getting defeated within seconds of landing.

Newly added points of interest, whether labeled or unlabeled on the map, always become popular landing locations. For example, at the start of Season 5, everyone wanted to check out and explore Paradise Palms, Lazy Links, and the other new unlabeled points of interest on the island.

When traveling together with one or more team-mates, don't walk (or run) too close together. This makes your group an easier target if enemies are hiding and waiting to launch a surprise attack.

Periodically check with your teammates and see who needs additional weapons, ammo, loot items, or resources. It's helpful if all teammates enter into a point of interest with their Health and Shield meters maxed out. Each soldier should also have the best arse-nal of weapons (with ammo) available to them.

If you know you're about to encounter an enemy squad, plan the best strategy based on the ter-rain. For example, one or two team members can approach from the front, while the other teammates plan a coordinated attack from the sides or from behind.

As a team, before launching an all-out assault against another group of enemies, assign one

player the job of sniper. Have that soldier hide in the high-ground in a location that has a clear line of sight to the attack zone. That soldier should set up a sniper's nest. Share weapons and ammo with that soldier so he or she is armed with plenty of long-range weaponry, including a rifle with a scope, as well as projectile explosive weapons that'll be able to destroy enemy fortresses.

As you travel as a group between points of inter-est, as long as you're not outrunning the storm, take the time to harvest resources along the way.

When a teammate gets injured and needs to be revived, don't just run up to offer help. The enemies that attacked your teammate will often stay in the area, hide, and wait to attack anyone who comes to provide assistance. Approach with caution.

When you're the teammate who gets injured, while waiting for a team member to revive you, try to crawl to a safe area, where enemy sol-diers can't easily attack you or your rescuer.

As soon as you're revived, consume an HP power-up, such as a Chug Jug, or use Bandages or a Med Kit to replenish your health and/or shields.

During a particularly intense firefight against enemy squads, if you see your teammates falling around you, first protect yourself and do what you can to defeat the enemy. Fend for yourself, and then when possible, revive your teammates. It's up to you to judge how much risk is involved to revive teammates and determine the best time to do this. If you, too, get defeated trying to revive others, you could all wind up being eliminated from a match.

Learn what skills your teammates have and take advantage of them. If one squad member has extraordinary aim when using a sniper rifle (or any gun with a scope), share weapons and ammo with that team member to ensure he or she has the items needed to take out enemies. Meanwhile, if another squad member is a particularly fast builder, put that person in charge of constructing and repairing forts for the team and keep that soldier flush with resources.

Each time you or someone in your party defeats an enemy, don't just brag and use emotes. Tell your team members what new weapons, ammo, loot items, and resources you've just acquired that the defeated enemy has left behind.

Defeating a single enemy is awesome, but in Duos or Squads mode, the enemy will often have squad mates nearby, and they'll want to avenge the demise of their team member, so be prepared for retaliation.

If you and your team are about to engage in battle against another multi-soldier squad, the element of surprise will always be in your favor. Try to divide the opposing squad and force the individual soldiers to fight alone against you and your teammates. Attempt to disrupt the opposing team's planned fighting strategies and cause as much confusion as possible.

Practice communicating and working together during matches. Anytime you're able to launch well-coordinated and perfectly timed attacks, you'll have an advantage.

CHAPTER 8

END GAME STRATEGIES THAT'LL HELP YOU SURVIVE THE FINAL CIRCLE

Depending on the gaming skill level of your-self and your squad member(s), hopefully some or all of you will eventually make it into the End Game of the matches you participate in. At this point, the more allies you have fight-ing alongside you, the better. However, with the right collection of weapons, ammo, loot items, and resources, it's possible to achieve #1 Victory Royale on your own, if necessary, even when you're playing in Duos or Squads mode.

After defeating an enemy, don't run up to grab what they've left behind unless you know it's safe. During the End Game, focus on quickly grabbing resources and health/shield power-ups, along with any weapons you know will be useful during the final minutes of a match.

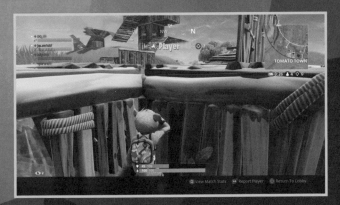

In between firefights, get somewhere safe and replenish your health and shields.

If you plan to rush an enemy fortress, have one of your teammates stay behind with a long-range weapon, and provide cover fire as you approach.

Once you're in the Final Circle, build up your fortress and try to maintain a height advantage over your opponents.

You can build an elaborate fortress, but if its base or mid-section is not sturdy, an enemy soldier will come along and shoot at the weak spots, causing the entire fortress to collapse with you in it.

When rushing an enemy base, as you approach, start throwing grenades or other explosive weapons to cause as much damage and disruption as possible—before you actually reach your destination and start shooting.

During the End Game, don't gather together in your base. One well-aimed explosive projectile weapon launched by an opponent could take out the entire squad with a single shot.

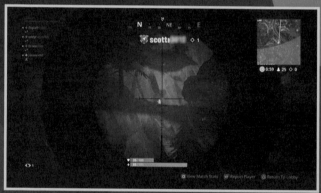

If you have a weapon that's equipped with an infrared scope, use it to see the heat signature of enemies who are hiding behind or within structures. The rifle the scope is attached to should provide the firepower needed to take out the enemy in your sights. If the enemy is within a structure, use a projectile explosive weapon to destroy the structure, and then quickly switch to the infrared scope rifle.

Staying close to the storm's edge could provide some level of protection but stay ahead of its movement. Always be prepared for an enemy to purposely go into the storm and reposition themselves behind you, so he/she can launch a surprise attack from behind when your attention is on the action happening in front of you. Here, the soldier is on the safe side of the storm, but just barely.

During the End Game, if you need to travel a good distance in order to stay within the circle, use a Launch Pad to catapult you into the sky, and then navigate your glider to the desired landing location. Anytime you discover a rift on the island, step into it. This sort of acts like a Launch Pad and immediately transports you elsewhere.

Study the terrain carefully. If you notice there's a lot of unusable or open terrain, try to anticipate the best location to establish your fortress, preferably at the top of a mountain or hill, so you have a natural height advantage. By looking at the Location Map, you can see that in addition to a lot of flat and open land, a portion of the circle covers the lake area. You never want to be within open water—especially during the End Game.

If time permits, climb to the top of the tallest hill or mountain to gain a height advantage within the circle. Just be careful about wasting resources you may need to build a fortress during the next skirmish.

While multiple allies can hang out around a single Cozy Campfire to replenish their health, make sure at least one person is standing guard, and that you're in a secure (enemy free) area. Clustering close together is rarely a good strategy.

The squad of enemies this soldier is fighting are at a disadvantage because they were hiding behind haystacks. As soon as their cover was blown, they were vulnerable to attack, because a haystack offers no protection whatsoever.

During this End Game, the pictured soldier has two of his squad mates by his side. Only two enemy soldiers remained, and the only visible fortress was empty. This soldier used his sniper rifle's scope to target all of the bushes where he figured out the remaining enemy soldiers were hiding. He then picked them off one at a time from the safety of his fortress.

More End Game Strategies

Here are twelve additional End Game strategies to help you win:

1. Choose the best location to build your fortress from which you'll make your final stand in battle. If you're in a good position, you can be more aggressive with your attacks. However, if you're in the dead-center of the Final Circle, you will become the center of attention, which probably isn't good.

2. Make sure your fortress is tall, well-fortified, and that it offers an excellent, 360-degree view of the surrounding area from the top level.

3. If your fortress gets destroyed, be prepared to move quick, and have a backup strategy in place that will help to ensure your survival. Having the element of surprise for your attacks gives you a tactical advantage. Don't become an easy target to hit—keep moving around your fort, or while you're out in the open!

4. During the End Game, don't engage every remaining player. Allow them to fight amongst themselves to reduce their numbers, plus reduce or even deplete their ammo and resources.

5. Only rely on a sniper rifle (or scoped rifle) to make long-range shots if you have really good aim and a clear line of sight to your enemy. Otherwise use explosive weapons that'll cause damage over a wide area. A Grenade Launcher, Guided Missile Launcher, or Rocket Launcher are ideal.

6. Always keep tabs on the location of your remaining enemies during the End Game. Don't allow them to sneak up behind you, for example. Even if your back is to the storm, an enemy could enter the storm temporarily, and then emerge behind you to launch a surprise attack if you lose track of their location. Gamers that use the storm to their

tactical advantage are referred to as "storm riders." If you lose track of an enemy who you know is nearby, listen carefully for their movement.

7. Don't invest a lot of resources in a massive and highly fortified fortress until you know you're in the Final Circle during a match. Refer to the map and the displayed timer. Otherwise, when the storm expands and moves, you could find it necessary to abandon your fort, and then need to build another one quickly, in a not-so-ideal location. Having to rebuild will use up your resources.

8. Base pushers are enemies that aren't afraid to leave their fortress and attempt to attack yours during the final minutes of a match. Be prepared to deal with their close-range threat.

9. If two or three enemies remain, focus on one at a time. Determine who appears to be the most imminent and largest threat. Be prepared to change priorities at a moment's notice, based on the actions of your enemies.

10. Some final battles take place on ramps, not from within fortresses. In this situation, speed/quick reflexes, getting higher up than your enemy, and good aim with the proper weapon are the keys to winning. Try to destroy the bottom of an enemy's ramp to make the whole thing come crashing down. The soldier standing on the ramp will be injured or defeated, based on how far he or she falls to the ground.

11. Have a Chug Jug on hand to replenish your health and shields if you're attacked, and incur damage, but are not defeated. Make sure you're well protected when you drink the Chug Jug. Med Kits are also great for maintaining HP during End Games.

12. Study the live streams created by expert *Fortnite* players (on YouTube and Twitch.tv) to learn their End Game strategies and see how they react to various challenges.

CHAPTER 9

FORTNITE: BATTLE ROYALE RESOURCES

There are two proven ways to become an awesome *Fortnite: Battle Royale* player. First, learn everything you can about the game and study how other expert players compete. Next, practice. When it comes to watching other players, four popular options include:

- Instead of leaving a match after you've been eliminated, stick around and watch the rest of each match in Spectator mode before returning to the Lobby.
- Watch pre-recorded YouTube videos produced by expert gamers that offer tips and advice, as well as detailed instruction. Just make sure the video applies to the most recent version of the game.
- Watch the live streams of highly ranked Fortnite: Battle Royale players on a service like YouTube Live or Twitch.tv.
- If Playground mode is active within the game (this is a feature that Epic Games periodically shuts down), spend time there exploring the island at your own pace without having to deal with the storm. Practice your building skills, learn all about the different terrain types on the island, and participate in mock fights with friends—without having to worry about being eliminated from a match.

On YouTube (www.youtube.com) or Twitch. TV (www.twitch.tv/directory/game/Fortnite), in the Search field, enter the search phrase "*Fortnite: Battle Royale*" to discover many game-related channels, live streams, and pre-recorded videos.

Also, be sure to check out these awesome online resources that will help you become a better *Fortnite: Battle Royale* player:

WEBSITE OR YOUTUBE CHANNEL NAME	DESCRIPTION	URL
Fandom's *Fortnite* Wiki	Discover the latest news and strategies related to *Fortnite: Battle Royale*.	http://fortnite.wikia.com/wiki/Fortnite_Wiki
FantasticalGamer	A popular YouTuber who publishes *Fortnite* tutorial videos.	www.youtube.com/user/FantasticalGamer
FBR Insider	The *Fortnite: Battle Royale Insider* website offers game-related news, tips, and strategy videos.	www.fortniteinsider.com
Fortnite Scout	Check your personal player stats, and analyze your performance using a bunch of colorful graphs and charts. Also check out the stats of other *Fortnite: Battle Royale* players.	www.fortnitescout.com
Fortnite Stats & Leaderboard	This is an independent website that allows you to view your own *Fortnite*-related stats or discover the stats from the best players in the world.	https://fortnitestats.com

(Continued on next page)

Game Informer Magazine's *Fortnite* Coverage	Discover articles, reviews, and news about *Fortnite: Battle Royale* published by *Game Informer* magazine.	www.gameinformer.com/search/searchresults.aspx?q=Fortnite
Game Skinny Online Guides	A collection of topic-specific strategy guides related to *Fortnite*.	www.gameskinny.com/tag/fortnite-guides/
GameSpot's *Fortnite* Coverage	Check out the news, reviews, and game coverage related to *Fortnite: Battle Royale* that's been published by GameSpot.	www.gamespot.com/fortnite
IGN Entertainment's *Fortnite* Coverage	Check out all IGN's past and current coverage of *Fortnite*.	www.ign.com/wikis/fortnite
Jason R. Rich's Website and Social Media Feeds	Share your *Fortnite: Battle Royale* game play strategies with this book's author and learn about his other books.	www.JasonRich.com www.FortniteGameBooks.com Twitter: @JasonRich7 Instagram: @JasonRich7
Microsoft's Xbox One *Fortnite* Website	Learn about and acquire *Fortnite: Battle Royale* if you're an Xbox One gamer.	www.microsoft.com/en-US/store/p/Fortnite-Battle-Royale/BT5P2X999VH2
MonsterDface YouTube and Twitch.tv Channels	Watch video tutorials and live game streams from an expert *Fortnite* player.	www.youtube.com/user/MonsterdfaceLive www.Twitch.tv/MonsterDface
Ninja	Check out the live and recorded game streams from Ninja, one of the most highly skilled *Fortnite: Battle Royale* players in the world, on Twitch.tv and YouTube.	www.twitch.tv/ninja_fortnite_hyper www.youtube.com/user/NinjasHyper
Nomxs	A YouTube and Twitch.tv channel hosted by online personality Simon Britton (Nomxs). He too is one of *Fortnite*'s top-ranked players.	https://youtu.be/np-8cmsUZmc or www.twitch.tv/videos/259245155
Official Epic Games YouTube Channel for *Fortnite: Battle Royale*	The official *Fortnite: Battle Royale* YouTube channel.	www.youtube.com/user/epicfortnite

Your *Fortnite: Battle Royale* Adventure Continues . . .

Hold onto your controller, keyboard, or touchscreen, because there's so much more new and exciting *Fortnite: Battle Royale* gaming in store for you as time goes on!

Epic Games continues to update this mega-popular game with sometimes dramatic alterations to the island map by introducing challenging new game play modes; by revealing exciting new storylines and subplots; by adding powerful new weapons and innovative types of new loot; and by making available eye-catching ways to showcase your soldier's appearance (with outfits, back bling, pickaxes, gliders, emotes, and other customizable elements).

To make sure that *Fortnite: Battle Royale* never becomes boring, predictable, or easy to master, new game play modes and competitions are introduced on a regular basis, while the Solo, Duos, and Squads modes continue to be tweaked to add new levels of challenges and excitement to them.

Plus, anytime you gather one or more friends to compete with you in the Duos or Squads game play modes, for example, the challenges and unpredictability within the game increase dramatically.

So, as the next Battle Bus departs with your soldier on it, good luck, and more importantly, have fun!